The Hebrew Yeshua vs. the Greek Jesus

New Light on the Seat of Moses from Shem-Tov's Hebrew Matthew

by

Nehemia Gordon

Preface by Avi Ben Mordechai

Foreword by Keith Johnson

Introduction by Michael Rood

Hilkiah Press

2005

Dedicated to my friend and student Reggie White.
May his love for the Word be an inspiration to us all.
תְּהִי נַפְשׁוֹ צְרוּרָה בִּצְרוֹר הַחַיִּים

Cover design by S. Kim Glassman

The cover of this book depicts: a "Moses' Seat" unearthed by archaeologists at the ancient synagogue of Chorazin, Israel; an excerpt of Greek Matthew from the Codex Sinaiticus; and an excerpt from a manuscript of Shem-Tov's Hebrew Matthew.

Second Edition

ISBN 0-9762637-0-X

Library of Congress Control Number: 2004114919

Copyright © 2005 by Nehemia Gordon, All Rights Reserved.
www.HebrewYeshua.com
www.HilkiahPress.com
hy@HilkiahPress.com

Table of Contents

Preface
by Avi Ben Mordechai

I had the privilege of meeting Nehemia Gordon in Jerusalem during the 2003 Hebrew festival of Sukkot. Although Nehemia is not a believer in Yeshua, he was speaking to a group of Torah-observant believers about some research he did on Matthew 23. Initially, I was not even planning to attend the lecture, but as divine destiny had it, I took a seat in the room and sat down to listen to him explain the subject for about two hours. After he presented his findings, I walked away awestruck. I had previously studied the Hebrew version of Matthew, but the manner and precision with which Gordon approached the subject was new. I found Gordon's methodology to be nothing short of scholarly. He had everything well documented, from ancient sources in their original languages of Hebrew, Aramaic, and Greek, but presented them in a manner understandable even by someone without a background in these languages.

Gordon starts off with the words of Yeshua in Matthew 23:2–3 that "the Pharisees sit in Moses' seat; all therefore whatsoever they bid you observe, that observe and do." On the surface this appears to be a New Testament commandment to obey the teachings of the Pharisees, tempered with a warning to avoid hypocrisy. Such a commandment coming from the mouth of Yeshua, appears to support the idea that today's Rabbis, who are an extension of the ancient Pharisees under a different label, must be obeyed.

In many Messianic circles, the question of Matthew 23:2–3 and how it pertains to Rabbinic (Pharisaic) authority has caused considerable division and disagreement. Some believe Yeshua was clear in what he said; that Rabbinic (Pharisaic) Judaism is valid and binding. For others, it is not so clear, believing his words to be, at the very least, misunderstood, or worse yet, corrupted. So, who is right? What is the correct way to understand Matthew 23:2–3, and what should be done with the Torah? Should it be followed? Obeyed? Or shunned?

Gordon answers these questions by placing Yeshua into his Hebraic context and allows Yeshua's own words to sparkle within their original Semitic setting. Gordon has opened the door to something that is going to have huge positive and long-lasting repercussions on present and future Messianic thought: something, in fact, that will leave its mark of truth on the hearts and minds of countless numbers of people!

Prepare yourself for a challenging ride of a lifetime, as you understand Yeshua and the New Testament through the lens of a strict Scripturalist. It is time for an accurate account of the real truth about the Hebrew Yeshua and the Greek Jesus. Enjoy!

Avi Ben Mordechai
Author and Lecturer in Understanding
Yeshua in a First-Century Hebraic Context
Millennium Communications
Jerusalem, Israel.

Foreword by Keith Johnson

As a Christian Pastor I am encouraged by reading *The Hebrew Yeshua versus the Greek Jesus.* Unfortunately many people will not get past the fact that the author is a Karaite *Jew.* I want to take this opportunity to challenge Christians to get past their prejudices about the messenger and focus on the message. By the way, I consider the messenger to be a great man in his own right.

When I met Nehemia Gordon in Israel, I was struck by his desire to not only study the Scriptures but more importantly his zeal to apply them into his life. I found out right away that he was not interested in "I think" theology. In other words, he was primarily focused on what was written in the Scriptures and not on how the church or synagogue interpreted them. This was a new concept for me as a seminary-educated pastor. Even though I was trained to "search the scriptures for myself" I soon realized that in many cases the English translation I was searching was not the same as the Hebrew Scriptures. I had to retrain myself to approach the Hebrew Scriptures as authority and not merely as a reference for "Christian living."

When interacting with Nehemia I was pushed to have a scriptural reference rather than a doctrinal or traditional interpretation. He wanted me to understand what was written for myself rather than being dependent on him or any other person. I started to better understand the passage in the book of Acts:

> Now the Bereans were of more noble character than the Thessalonians, for they searched the scriptures daily to see if what Paul said was true. (Acts 17:11)

Nehemia left his life in American culture and immersed himself in the life and culture of Israel. In the same way, Nehemia's book invites us to walk a similar journey. We have an opportunity to enter into the life, language and culture of Yeshua of Nazareth.[1] Nehemia has presented the church a *gift* by writing about the message of Yeshua.

The timing of publication could not be better. It was considered by some as radical and unconventional when Mel Gibson decided to make his movie *The Passion of the Christ* in the "foreign" languages of Latin, Aramaic, and Hebrew with English subtitles. I could not believe how many "Bible-believing Christians" were caught off guard when they realized that "Jesus" didn't speak English. They were even in shock when they found out his name wasn't Jesus in the First Century. It showed me how far removed the church is from the language and culture of Yeshua of Nazareth.

My prayer is that people of all faiths will take the time to open the gift of this book and read the message that will send us back to the first message from heaven: the Torah!

Keith Johnson
Charlotte, North Carolina

[1] Yeshua is an abbreviation of the biblical name Yehoshua יְהוֹשֻׁעַ.

Introduction by Michael Rood

The Israeli New Moon Society convened without fanfare as the mixed rumblings of Yiddish, Spanish, and English faded, and the host opened the meeting in the only language appropriate for addressing Biblical topics; Hebrew. The room was filled with men in black coats and hats who wore curling side-locks that drew down into full beards. Interspersed in the crowd was an occasional multi-colored *kippah* marking those who were more modern, yet unmistakably Orthodox in persuasion. We were gathered to discuss the ancient Biblical Hebrew Calendar.

The keynote speaker prepared his notes on the dais and then quickly walked back to my table. After a brief introduction, he scribbled a name and telephone number on a minuscule corner of a piece of notepaper and covered the small scrap with his thumb and said; "You need to contact this person as soon as possible. Now, don't let anyone see this name or it will get both of us thrown out of here – do you understand?" I nodded and he lifted his thumb. Sliding the scrap to the edge of the desk, I rolled it into a tube and stuck it in my pocket. The next day I was sitting in a coffee shop in downtown Jerusalem with the person whose name was covertly etched on the paper, Nehemia Gordon. I was about to learn why this man was both respected and feared among the Orthodox religious community in Jerusalem.

Nehemia related to me that he was raised in America – the son of an Orthodox rabbi. He began attending Hebrew school and learning Torah (the five books of Moses) at an early age. As his education progressed, he began studying the Talmud and other writings of the Jewish sages. The more questions he asked of his rabbis, the less satisfying their answers became. He discovered through his rabbis that he was asking the same questions raised by the Karaites in the middle ages. "Karaites?" I asked, "What is a Karaite?"

When Jerusalem was destroyed in the year 70 of the Common Era, the Temple service that had described Judaism for over a thousand years was abruptly brought to an end. Hundreds of thousands of Jews were mercilessly slaughtered by the Romans. The priesthood was in disarray, and the Pharisees (with the permission of Rome) stepped in to fill the spiritual vacancy that was left by the priests of Zadok. Out of the national chaos that developed at that time, the Pharisees, who were a relatively small religious group up to that point, redefined the practices of Judaism and developed a new religious system. Throughout the synagogues of the Diaspora, new practices, rules, regulations, and codes of righteousness were imposed upon the followers of the Pharisees. These were eventually codified in the writings of the Talmud. The Pharisee leaders, called "Rabbis" (great ones), claimed *divine* authority to establish these new innovations. As Phariseeism grew, Jews who held fast to the Scriptures and refused to accept either the authority or the innovations of the Rabbis, became commonly known as "Karaites" or "Scripturalists." Before Phariseeism emerged, the term "Karaite" was unknown and unnecessary.

As Nehemia delineated to me the principles of historic Karaism, he quoted the same passages from the prophets that Yeshua (Jesus) had quoted when he himself contested the authority of the Pharisees. Nehemia also chided the Pharisees on some of the same issues for which Yeshua himself reproved them. I said to myself, "Yeshua sounds like a Karaite!" Nehemia suggested that we meet again the following day to continue our discussion. I couldn't resist.

We arranged ourselves at a quiet indoor table at the same cafe the following afternoon. In the course of our conversation, Nehemia learned that I was Messianic (a Jew who believes that Yeshua of Nazareth is the Messiah). He made it clear to me that, while as a Karaite he does not believe that Yeshua is the Messiah, he has, as part of his studies, read the New Testament. Nehemia inquired about my "take" on the New Testament. Considering his familiarity with the New Testament and expertise in the **T**a**N**a**Ch** (Hebrew acronym for **T**orah – five books of Moses, **N**evi'im – prophets, and **Ch**etuvim – writings) I knew that I could relate my perspective in about an hour.

At the end of my monologue, Nehemia rocked back in his chair, shook his head incredulously and exclaimed, "The way you're describing Yeshua makes him sound like a Karaite!" Nehemia and I had, in our own experiences, both identified with the same principles expressed by the Karaites; me through my embrace of Yeshua's teachings and my rejection of "paganized-Christian" traditions – and Nehemia through his embrace of the TaNaCh and his rejection of "Pharisaic-Jewish" traditions. Coming from two different worlds, we identified with each other. We became friends.

While my initial contact with Nehemia came about through our respective work on the Biblical Hebrew Calendar, over the past several years he has been an invaluable resource to me in the course of my Biblical investigations here in the land of Israel. His experience in the field of ancient Biblical texts is extraordinary. He is fluent in both ancient and Modern Hebrew and reads various dialects of Aramaic, Syriac, and Greek. Nehemia has also worked as a translator on the Dead Sea Scrolls.

In the fall of 2001, I went to Nehemia with what I suspected to be a textual problem in the Gospel of Matthew. I described the problem in detail and asked if he would use his linguistic and textual skills as a scholar of ancient texts to find an answer. Nehemia's search for a solution eventually led him to an ancient text of the Gospel of Matthew – **in Hebrew**.

Early church fathers recorded that Matthew wrote his Gospel in the Hebrew language, and it was subsequently translated into other languages. It was believed that most of the Hebrew texts of Matthew were expunged during Roman persecutions of the followers of Yeshua, but, as it turns out, ancient Hebrew texts of Matthew were clandestinely preserved and copied by Jewish scribes. These texts were copied in secret, because the Roman Catholic Church forbade Jews to possess copies of New Testament books – especially Hebrew versions of these books. Miraculously, some of these original language texts of Matthew's Gospel were preserved down through modern times and are now available to Hebrew scholars.

As Nehemia compared the Greek translation of Matthew's Gospel to the ancient Hebrew text, he was astonished at the clarity of Yeshua words in the original Hebrew language. The Greek text contained common 'Hebrew to Greek' translation errors that have caused the words of Yeshua to become critically distorted from what was accurately recorded in Hebrew. Yeshua's brutally honest and precisely chosen words in the Hebrew version of Matthew are nothing less than revolutionary. This is the revelation for which **I** have been waiting an entire lifetime!

You are about to embark on a journey of discovery that will break the shackles of religious bondage and set you free from the manipulation of man-made religion. You hold in your hands a multifaceted gem of life-changing truth. Set aside at least three uninterrupted hours for this adventure. Don't put it off. Take the phone off the hook and bolt the doors. Nehemia "The Karaite" Gordon is going to take you to the ruins of the Chorazin synagogue in the Galilee, sit you upon "The Seat of Moses," and show you one of the greatest Biblical discoveries of modern times.

Michael Rood
Jerusalem, Israel

Chapter 1
Whatsoever They Bid You Observe...

The present study may seem surprising coming from a Karaite Jew. The word Karaite means "Hebrew Scripturalist" and by definition Karaites are strictly *Tanach* or what some people call "Old Testament." My motto is, "If it's not in the Tanach [Old Testament], I can't use it." So why would a Karaite who does not believe in Jesus or Yeshua[2] write a study on the Gospel of Matthew? Well in the past few years I have gone on an unexpected journey of discovery I feel compelled to share. In retrospect, my background as a Karaite probably paved the way for me to ask questions that a non-Karaite might not have

[2] In this study I have used the name "Yeshua" merely as a matter of convention without any intention of promoting one particular pronunciation or another. Note that in my quotations of the Hebrew Matthew below, the Rabbinical acronym *Ye.sh.u.* יֵשׁ״וּ which stands for ***y**imach **sh**emo **v**ezichro* יִמַּח שְׁמוֹ וְזִכְרוֹ "may his name and memory be blotted out" has been restored to Yeshu[a] ישו[ע], which historically is the late Hebrew abbreviated form of *Yehoshua* יְהוֹשֻׁעַ "Joshua" (see Nehemiah 8:17 in Hebrew where Joshua son of Nun is called *Yeshua* יֵשׁוּעַ). All quotations from ancient sources in this study have been translated directly from the ancient languages by myself except where otherwise noted.

bothered asking and to challenge assumptions that a non-Karaite would likely have taken for granted. I pray that by sharing this information I am glorifying the name of Yehovah, the most high 'El, Creator of heaven and earth and His perfect Torah.

It all started when my friend Michael Rood, a Messianic teacher, asked me what I thought of Matthew 23:1–3. Michael explained that in this passage Yeshua told his disciples to obey the Pharisees because they teach with authority. At first I told Michael that as a Karaite I stick to the Tanach and therefore I did not really have an opinion on the matter. Michael asked me if I could nevertheless use my scholarly training to help him understand this text. I hold a degree in Archaeology and Biblical studies from the Hebrew University of Jerusalem and have worked for several years on the Dead Sea Scroll Publication Project, the official publication of the Dead Sea Scrolls. So Michael figured I could use these skills to try and shed some light on the book of Matthew.

I told Michael that before I agreed to research the issue I would need to better understand the problem. If the problem were simply that he did not like what it said in Matthew 23 then there was probably not much I could do to help. Michael began to explain by opening up to Matthew 23:2–3 and reading to me from the King James Version:

> (2) The scribes and the Pharisees sit in Moses' seat: (3) All therefore whatsoever they bid you observe, that observe and do; but do not ye after their works: for they say, and do not. (Matthew 23:2–3 [KJV])

Michael explained that Yeshua seemed to be saying that the Pharisees teach with authority because they sit in Moses' seat. I was not familiar with the concept of "Moses' seat" and asked Michael what it meant. He explained that there were two main opinions on the meaning of the phrase "Moses' seat." Some said that in every synagogue there was an actual chair called a "Moses'

Seat" in which the leaders of the congregation would sit and teach with authority.[3] The other opinion was that "Moses' seat" was a figure of speech indicating someone who teaches with the authority of Moses.[4] Either way, the statement that the Pharisees sit in "Moses' seat" meant that they have some kind of Mosaic authority. Matthew seemed to be saying that the words of the Pharisees should be followed but because they are hypocrites their actions should not be emulated. The implication is that a true follower of Yeshua would need to do whatever the Pharisees taught, in order to faithfully obey Yeshua's instructions. In practice this would mean following all the rules and regulations which the Pharisees invented without any Scriptural basis. I knew all about these rules and regulations because I was raised as an Orthodox Rabbinical Jew, in essence a modern-day Pharisee. I vividly remember being taught these rules and regulations out of

[3] The front cover of this book depicts a ritual chair found by archaeologists at the ancient synagogue of Chorazin in the Galilee which they believe to be a "Moses' Seat." Similar ritual chairs were also found at the ancient synagogues of Hammat Tiberias, Ein Gedi, Delos, and Dura Europos (Sukenik pp. 57–61; Davies and Allison p. 268; Renov; but see Rahmani). The phrase "Moses' Seat" *ketidra demoshe* קָתֶדְרָא דְמֹשֶׁה is also mentioned in the 5th Century Rabbinical Midrash *Pesikta DeRav Kahana* 1:7 [Mandelbaum ed. p. 12]). On the date and character of this Midrash see Strack and Stemberger p. 322. For a related reference see also *Exodus Rabbah* §43:4.

[4] The metaphorical interpretation of "Moses' Seat" as Mosaic authority seems likely. It is a basic Pharisaic doctrine that the Rabbis have the authority of Moses. This is expressed in the well-known Talmudic account about the dispute between Rabban Gamaliel II and Rabbi Joshua. These two rabbis disagreed about when Yom Kippur was to fall in a certain year, but Rabban Gamaliel sat on the Rabbinic court, and hence Rabbi Joshua was compelled to accept his ruling even though he knew it to be factually wrong. Rabbi Dosa reasoned to Rabbi Joshua that he must give in to Gamaliel's ruling because:

> If we go and challenge Rabban Gamaliel's court, we must also challenge each and every court that has presided since the days of Moses until now… <u>each and every set of three [Rabbis] that preside as a court over Israel are equivalent to the court of Moses</u>. (*Babylonian Talmud*, Rosh Hashannah 25a).

So the Rabbis really believed they preside in place of Moses!

the *Shulchan Aruch*, the modern Rabbinical treatise which covers every aspect of daily life down to its finest details.[5] One of the rules that stuck in my head was the instruction on how to put on one's shoes in the morning:

> A person must first put on his right shoe, but not tie it. Then he must put on his left shoe and tie it and go back and tie his right shoe. (*Shulchan Aruch*, Orach Chayim 2:4)[6]

Rabbi Moshe Isserles, the Ashkenazic Rabbi who annotated the *Shulchan Aruch* with traditions unique to European Jews adds:

> Note: Even with our shoes, which do not have laces, a person must still put on his right shoe first. (*Shulchan Aruch*, Orach Chayim 2:4)

I sympathized with Michael: had Yeshua really commanded him to listen to the Pharisees tell him how to put on his shoes? Yet this seemed to be the plain meaning of Yeshua's words, "whatsoever they bid you observe, that observe and do." I said to Michael that I understood his dilemma but if this is what Yeshua taught then perhaps he ought to obey the Pharisees. I did not see what the problem was, other than that Michael might die of heat exhaustion wearing modern Pharisaic garb in the Jerusalem heat. As I said this I could not help but laugh at my own joke. The problem, Michael explained, was that if you read the rest of

[5] The *Shulchan Aruch* was written in the 16th Century by a Sephardic Jew named Joseph Caro. Back then the Pharisees were sharply split between Sephardim who lived in Muslim countries and Ashkenazim who lived in Christian countries. At first, Joseph Caro's book was shunned by the Ashkenazim because it only documented Sephardic practices. But then Rabbi Moshe Isserles, an Ashkenazic Rabbi, added his "notes" which delineated how the Ashkenazic tradition differed from the Sephardic and overnight the *Shulchan Aruch* was transformed into a universally accepted guide to daily Pharisaic living.

[6] *Shulchan Aruch* vol. 1 p. 11.

Matthew 23 Yeshua is warning his disciples ***not*** to follow the errors of the Pharisees. For example,

> But woe unto you, scribes and Pharisees, hypocrites! for ye shut up the kingdom of heaven against men: for ye neither go in yourselves, neither suffer ye them that are entering to go in. (Matthew 23:13 [KJV])

Could Yeshua really be telling his disciples to obey these Pharisees who "shut up the kingdom of heaven against men"?! Michael read me another verse:

> Woe unto you, scribes and Pharisees, hypocrites! for ye are like unto whited sepulchres, which indeed appear beautiful outward, but are within full of dead men's bones, and of all uncleanness. (Matthew 23:27 [KJV])

Yeshua describes the Pharisees as tombs which contain every type of uncleanness in them. Could Yeshua really be telling his followers to obey the instructions of those he was calling hypocrites and whited sepulchres?

I told Michael I was still not convinced. Perhaps Yeshua recognized the Rabbinical prerogative to invent new laws, but was accusing them of not following their own man-made rules. This certainly seemed to be the meaning of the passage in English. Michael said there was another reason he had a hard time accepting that Yeshua would instruct his disciples to obey the Pharisees. In Matthew 15 there was a story about the disciples sitting down to eat bread and not washing their hands. The Pharisees complained to Yeshua that his disciples were violating the traditions of the elders and Yeshua responded that it was the Pharisees who were violating the Torah by imposing these man-made traditions.

Chapter 2
Washing the Hands

I had come into contact with Yeshua's teaching against the traditions of the elders some years before. Back then I met a very interesting fellow who described himself as a "Torah-keeping Christian." I had never met a Torah-keeping Christian before and was quite perplexed at what this might mean. I had always thought that the followers of Yeshua hated the Torah, that they believed the Torah had been done away with and "nailed to the cross." So when this new friend of mine revealed to me he was a Torah-keeping Christian I asked him to explain what he meant. He had spent some time with me and he knew that whenever you discuss anything with a Karaite you must bring your sources. So rather than talk in theory he simply opened up his New Testament to the book of Matthew and read me the words of Yeshua:

> For verily I say unto you, Till heaven and earth pass, one jot or one tittle shall in no wise pass from the law, till all be fulfilled. (Matthew 5:18 [KJV])

He explained that Yeshua was saying the Torah was not done away with, not even in the minutest detail. And then my friend continued, "But…". There's always a "but" in these things. "But," my Torah-keeping Christian friend explained, "there were some things in the Torah that Yeshua did do away with." Well, I knew it was too good to be true. I asked him if he could give me some examples. He explained that there had originally been a commandment to wash the hands before eating bread but Yeshua did away with this commandment. When I heard this I could not help but crack a grin. I asked my friend to open up to the verse in the "Old Testament" where it said to wash the hands before eating bread. He was sure it was there somewhere… must be in Leviticus or Numbers, somewhere with all those "ritual" laws. I let him squirm for awhile as he skimmed chapter after chapter. After about 15 minutes I explained to him that there was no such commandment anywhere in the Torah.

Washing the hands before eating bread was a sensitive topic for me. I was raised as a strict Orthodox Rabbinical Jew, my father being an Orthodox rabbi himself. Growing up, I was taught that it is a great sin to eat bread without first "washing the hands." When the Rabbis talk about "washing the hands" they do not mean to take a bar of soap and cleanse oneself: that's just common-sense hygiene. What the Rabbis mean is a very specific ritual-washing of the hands. The Rabbinical ritual begins with a special jug that fulfills certain requirements and specifications. This jug is filled with water and then placed in the right hand and used to pour water over the left hand. Then the jug is passed to the left hand and water is poured over the right hand. The process is repeated a second time and according to some traditions a third time. At the end, a blessing must be recited:

> Blessed art thou Lord, king of the universe, who has sanctified us with His commandments **and commanded us to wash the hands**.[7]

When I was growing up and faced this ritual on a daily basis, I began to object to this blessing, because as far as I could tell there was no such commandment in the Torah. My rabbis explained to me that the practice of washing the hands was a Rabbinical "enactment" and God had commanded us to obey the Rabbis. By obeying this Rabbinical enactment we were supposedly obeying God who commanded us to obey the Rabbis. When I asked to see where God tells us to obey the Rabbis I was told to stop asking so many questions.

Well, I knew that washing the hands was nowhere to be found in the Torah and I explained this to my Torah-keeping Christian friend. He was surprised so we opened up Matthew 15 where it tells how Yeshua's disciples sit down to eat bread without washing their hands. Yeshua is approached by the Pharisees who complain to him:

> (2) Why do thy disciples transgress the **tradition of the elders**? for they wash not their hands when they eat bread. (3) But he answered and said unto them, Why do ye also transgress the **commandment of God** by your tradition? (Matthew 15:2–3 [KJV])

Yeshua's disciples were not accused of violating the Torah but rather of violating the "tradition of the elders." Yeshua responded that it was actually the traditions of the elders that

[7] The blessing in Hebrew is:

בָּרוּךְ אַתָּה אֲדֹנָי אֱלֹהֵינוּ מֶלֶךְ הָעוֹלָם, אֲשֶׁר קִדְּשָׁנוּ בְּמִצְוֹתָיו וְצִוָּנוּ עַל נְטִילַת יָדָיִם

See *Babylonian Talmud*, Berachot 60b; *Shulchan Aruch*, Orach Chayim 4:1 [vol. 1 p. 15]; *Siddur Rinat Yisrael* (modern Rabbinic prayer book) p. 108. The rules of washing the hands are detailed in *Kitzur Shulchan Aruch* §40 [Basel ed. pp. 223–231; Goldin Translation pp. 125–130].

transgress the commandment of God. I can understand how someone unfamiliar with Phariseeism might confuse "tradition of the elders" with Torah. But I grew up with Phariseeism and in a way I understood exactly what Yeshua was talking about because I went through the same thing myself. I realized that in order to understand what Yeshua was saying my friend needed a crash course in Pharisaic Judaism.

Chapter 3
Understanding Phariseeism

I began to explain to my friend that the modern Orthodox Rabbis were the continuation of the ancient Pharisees; it says that right in the Talmud.[8] Of course, after 2000 years there have been some changes, but essentially both the Pharisees and Rabbis adhere to the same five fundamental principles which I call the "Five Iniquities of the Rabbis."

Iniquity #1: Two Torahs

The first of these fundamental principles is perhaps the most important and far-reaching. This is the doctrine that when Moses ascended Mt. Sinai he received two Torahs, an Oral Torah and a written Torah. This is a very ancient concept, which the Talmud cites in the name of Shammai, a famous rabbi who lived a few decades before Yeshua:

> Our Rabbis taught: An incident with a certain gentile that came before Shammai. He said to him: How many

[8] *Babylonian Talmud*, Kidushin 66a; Nidah 33b.

> Torahs do you have? [Shammai] answered: Two, the Written Torah and the Oral Torah (*Torah She-Be'al Peh* תּוֹרָה שֶׁבְּעַל פֶּה). (*Babylonian Talmud,* Sabbath 31a)

So, the most fundamental doctrine of Phariseeism is the belief in the Oral Torah, sometimes called the "Oral Law." The Talmud explains that this "Oral" Torah was revealed to Moses in a second revelation at Mt. Sinai.[9] According to the Midrash, this "second" Torah was given orally to keep it out of the hands of the Gentiles. God knew that the Tanach ("Old Testament") would be translated into Greek, explains the Midrash, so He gave the Oral Law by word of mouth to preserve it as the exclusive domain of the Rabbis as a sort of secret knowledge.[10]

[9] The Pharisaic doctrine of the second revelation at Sinai appears in the following Talmudic passage:

> Rabbi Levy bar Chama said in the name of Rabbi Simeon ben Lakish: What is meant by the verse: 'And I will give you the tablets of stone, the law, and the commandment which I have written to teach them.' (Exodus 24:12). *Tablets* refers to the ten commandments; *law* refers to the Torah; *and the commandment* refers to the Mishnah; *which I have written* refers to the Prophets and the Writings; *to teach them* refers to the Talmud. This teaches us that all of them were given to Moses at Sinai. (*Babylonian Talmud*, Berachot 5a).

The doctrine of the second revelation also appears in the Midrash:

> When the Almighty revealed Himself at Sinai in order to give the Torah to Israel, he recited to Moses in due order the Scriptures, the Mishnah, the Talmud and the Midrash... **Even that which a student asks his Rabbi, did the Almighty tell over to Moses at that time.** After he learned it from the mouth of the Almighty, [Moses] said: 'Master of the universe! Let me write it for them.' [The Almighty] replied: 'I do not wish to give it to them [entirely] in writing... but the Scriptures do I give to them in writing while the Mishnah, the Talmud, and the Midrash I give to them orally.' (*Exodus Rabbah* §47:1 [compare Lehrman Translation p. 536])

[10] The Pharisaic doctrine of the Oral Law as a secret knowledge given to the Rabbis appears in the following Midrashic passage:

One of the most profound changes in Phariseeism since the 1st Century CE is that the Oral Torah has been written down. The first to begin writing it down was Rabbi Judah the Prince, who in about 200 CE wrote down the *Mishnah*, a compilation of Pharisaical doctrines and practices discussed in the rabbinical academies. During the following centuries the Rabbis debated the meaning of various Mishnaic passages and these debates and explanations were written down as the Talmud. There are actually two Talmuds. The Jerusalem Talmud was written in Tiberias and completed around the year 350; it was named "Jerusalem" Talmud even though it was written in Tiberias to give it more prestige. The Jerusalem Talmud is usually referred to in English as the "Palestinian Talmud." The second Talmud was completed around the year 500 CE by Ravina and Rav Ashi in Babylonia and was called the **Babylonian Talmud.**[11] In the Middle Ages, the Jerusalem Talmud was largely ignored while the Babylonian Talmud gained a position of authority. Today, when rabbis speak about "Talmud" without specifying which one, they mean the Babylonian Talmud. The third part of the Oral Law is the Midrash which was written down from the 2nd–9th Centuries CE.[12]

> [God] said to [Moses], I do not want to give it to them in writing, because it is known to Me that the idolaters will rule over them in the future and will take [Scripture] from them and it will be despised by the idolaters. Therefore I am giving them Scripture in writing, but the Mishnah, the Talmud, and the Midrash I give to them orally, so when the idolaters come and [Israel] is subjugated by them, [Israel] will still remain separate from them. (*Exodus Rabbah* §47:1 [compare Lehrman Translation p. 536])

[11] From the time of the Babylonian exile in the 6th Century BCE up until 1956 CE there was always a large thriving Jewish community in Babylonia. In 1956 the Arab state of Iraq forcibly expelled the entire community of Babylonian Jews who ironically had been there longer than the Arabs themselves.

[12] Among the earliest *Midrashim* is *Seder Olam Rabbah* which dates to the 2nd Century CE. One of the latest *Midrashim* is *Pirkei deRebbi Eliezer* dating to the 9th Century.

While the *Mishnah* and *Talmud* are arranged by topic, the *Midrash* is arranged as a running commentary on biblical verses.

Iniquity #2: Authority of the Rabbis

The second fundamental principle of Rabbinic/ Pharisaic Judaism is the belief that the Rabbis have **absolute authority** to interpret Scripture, and what they say in religious matters is binding, even if it is known to be factually untrue. This is best expressed by the Rabbinical doctrine that if the Rabbis say right is left or left is right you must obey them.[13] When I was growing up this was a problem I faced on a daily basis. I would constantly be coming to my rabbis and protesting that this or that "interpretation" in the Talmud seemed to fly in the face of the explicit words of Scripture. I was told time and again that the Rabbis have interpreted it this way and we had no right to question it.

One day, one of my rabbis sat me down to convince me of the absolute authority of the Rabbis. He began to tell me the story of Rabbi Eliezer which appears in the *Babylonian Talmud*, tractate Baba Metsia, page 59b. Rabbi Eliezer was the greatest of the Rabbinical sages and the teacher of the legendary Rabbi Akiva. One day Rabbi Eliezer was engaged in a debate with the rest of the rabbis on some minutia of rabbinical law. Rabbi Eliezer maintained that a certain type of oven could not contract

[13] The Midrash states concerning the authority of the Rabbis:

> Even if they instruct you that right is left or left is right, you must obey them. (*Sifre Deuteronomy* §154 on Deuteronomy 17:11 [Finkelstein ed. p. 207; compare Hammer Translation p. 190]).

See also Rashi on Deuteronomy 17:11 [Mosad Harav Cook ed. p. 151; Isaiah and Sharfman Translation p. 163]. Of this the prophet spoke, "Woe to those that call evil, good and good, evil, that call darkness, light and light, darkness, that call bitter, sweet and sweet, bitter." (Isaiah 5:20)

ritual uncleanness while all the other rabbis said it could.[14] The Talmud relates that "On that day R. Eliezer brought forward every imaginable argument" but he could not convince the other rabbis. Rabbi Eliezer became very frustrated. His rational arguments clearly proved he was right but this was not enough to convince the other rabbis to change their ruling. What was he to do? In desperation Rabbi Eliezer invoked a miracle. He shouted out, "If I am right, let the trees prove it!" All the rabbis in the academy suddenly heard a great rumble and when they looked outside they saw an entire orchard of trees inexplicably being uprooted and flying into the air. The rabbis were very impressed but they turned to Rabbi Eliezer and said, "We do not listen to trees." Rabbi Eliezer tried again. He shouted out: "If I am right let the river prove it!" Everyone in the academy ran outside and witnessed as the great river began to flow backwards. The rabbis were now extremely impressed but they turned to Rabbi Eliezer and said, "We do not listen to rivers." Rabbi Eliezer was by now steaming at the collar and shouted, "If I am right let the walls of the academy prove it." The walls of the academy immediately began to cave in. The rabbis turned to Rabbi Eliezer and said: "We do not listen to walls." Rabbi Eliezer was at his wits' end and finally shouted out, "If the law agrees with me, let it be proved from Heaven!" At that moment all those present in the academy heard a voice call out from heaven saying: "Why do you dispute with Rabbi Eliezer, seeing that in all matters the law agrees with him!" The rabbis were again impressed but turned to Rabbi Eliezer and said, "Sorry, we do not listen to Heaven." As my rabbi was telling me this story he opened to Deuteronomy 30:12 which says concerning the Torah "it is not in heaven." Of course, this phrase is part of a verse that says there is no excuse not to

[14] The story of Rabbi Eliezer is commonly known as "The Oven of 'Achnai" after this special type of oven.

follow the Torah because it is not in heaven or across the sea but in our hearts and mouths. The Israelites had just heard the Torah directly from Moses and knew exactly what it meant, so there could be no excuses not to live by it. But this same verse was brought by the Rabbis as proof to Rabbi Eliezer why they should not listen to the Creator in matters of Torah. Once the Torah was given it was no longer in heaven and therefore God had no say in interpreting it. My rabbi's conclusion from all this was that **the interpretations of the Rabbis even superseded a direct decree from God Himself**, so who was I to question them. When my rabbi finished explaining these things to me I turned to him and thanked him. I told him that that was all I needed to hear. Until then I had had my doubts about the Oral Law and the Rabbis, but now I knew for certain that this was not of God.

Later, when I was older, I read this same story about Rabbi Eliezer directly out of the Talmud and found that it had a continuation. After the face off between the Rabbis and Rabbi Eliezer, one of the Rabbis was wandering through the forest when he met the prophet Elijah (the Rabbis believe that Elijah never died and that he often communicates with them).[15] This particular Rabbi asked Elijah what God said when he heard the rabbis of the academy proclaim that they do not listen to heaven. Elijah revealed that at that moment the Creator laughed and said: *banai nitschuni banai nitschuni* בָּנַי נִצְּחוּנִי בָּנַי נִצְּחוּנִי "My Sons have defeated me! My sons have defeated me!" (*Babylonian Talmud*, Baba Metsia 59b).[16]

Iniquity #3: Irrational Interpretation

The third iniquity of the Rabbis is their use of *irrational interpretation*. The Torah tells us exactly how we are to understand

[15] Indeed, at Rabbinical circumcisions they leave an empty chair for Elijah and on Passover eve there is a tradition to open the door to let in Elijah!

[16] For more on the incident of Rabbi Eliezer, see Appendix 3.

its words. In Deuteronomy 31 there is a commandment that the entire nation of Israel – the men, the women, the children, and the stranger in the gates – must gather on the Feast of Booths (Tabernacles) every seventh year and hear the Torah read to them. The purpose of this public reading of the Torah is so that the Israelites would hear, learn, and do the Torah:

> "(12) Gather the nation, the men, the women, the children, and the sojourner in your gates, in order that they **hear**, and in order that they **learn** and fear YHWH your God and **diligently do** all the words of this Torah. (13) And their children who did not know, they shall hear and learn to fear YHWH your God…" (Deuteronomy 31:12–13)

The purpose of this public reading was to teach Torah to the average person who would hear, learn, and do. We have to remember that in ancient times, long before the printing press, the average person did not have a Torah in his house. In order to produce a copy of the Torah a person had to have the resources to slaughter an entire flock of sheep to produce parchment and then pay a scribe to sit for about a year and painstakingly write an accurate copy of the Torah. This is why the king is commanded in Deuteronomy 17:18 to write for himself a copy of the Torah; as Israel's king he needs the Torah as a constant guide of how to rule so he must have a copy at hand. But the average Israelite could not afford his own Torah, so his main access to the divine instruction was at the public reading every seventh year.

What we learn from Deuteronomy 31 is that the Torah was written in such a way that it would be completely comprehensible to these ancient Israelites, by simply hearing it. When we interpret Scripture today we have to place ourselves in the position of those ancient Israelites as they heard the Torah read to them. Of course, we have unique challenges they did not have. We must span a gap of 3500 years of culture and language. Although

Hebrew is a spoken language in modern Israel, the Hebrew of Scripture is quite different and we must understand the language as it was used when the Torah was given. Once we span the cultural and linguistic gaps, we must ask ourselves: "In the time of Moses, how would the ancient Israelites have understood the Torah?" Any interpretation not obvious to an ancient Israelite shepherd listening in the public reading cannot be what is intended by Torah.

The problem is that the Rabbis interpret Scripture using what is known today as *midrashic* interpretation.[17] *Midrashic* interpretation consists of taking words out of context and reading meaning into them. A good example of this is Exodus 23:2 which says:

> "You shall not go after the majority to do evil, neither shall you testify in a matter of strife to incline after the majority to pervert justice" (Exodus 23:2)

What this verse means is that we should not testify that a person is guilty just because everyone else says he is guilty; this would be a perversion of justice. We must testify to the truth whatever that happens to be, even if we are the lone voice of reason. The Rabbis take this same verse and derive a completely different principle from it. They arbitrarily remove words from the beginning and end of the verse, as such:

> "~~You shall not go after the majority to do evil, neither shall you testify in a matter of strife to~~ incline after the majority ~~to pervert justice~~" (Exodus 23:2)[18]

[17] "Midrashic" interpretation is also sometimes called in English, "hermeneutical" or "homiletical" interpretation.

[18] *Babylonian Talmud*, Baba Metsia 59b. The "commandment" to follow the majority of rabbis is actually a fundamental concept in Phraiseeism. Maimonides explains that if there is a debate on an interpretation of any law between 1001 rabbis and

What is left is "incline after the majority." Disembodied from their original context, these words are "interpreted" as a commandment to "go after the majority." Whatever the majority of rabbis says is binding because Exodus 23:2 says to go after the majority. Never mind that Exodus 23:2 actually says **not to go** after the majority but to go after **whatever is true**. This does not matter because the Rabbis have the prerogative to "interpret" as they see fit. This practice of taking words out of context and twisting their meaning is typical of the Rabbinical approach to Scripture. Strictly speaking this approach is not "interpretive" but rather "creative." It uses random sound bites to create new meaning not naturally emanating from the words of Scripture.

Iniquity #4: Traditions of Men

The fourth iniquity of the Rabbis is the sanctification of tradition or folk customs. The Rabbis believe that if something is done by an entire Jewish community for an extended period of time, then this custom, called *minhag* מִנְהָג, becomes binding upon the community. This principle is enshrined in the Rabbinical maxim *minhag yisrael torah hi* מִנְהָג יִשְׂרָאֵל תּוֹרָה הִיא "A custom of Israel is a law." Actually, it literally says, "A custom of Israel is **Torah**"![19] A classic example of this is the wearing of the *kippah* or skullcap. This was a practice unknown in Talmudic times.[20] In the Middle Ages a custom developed to cover the head and after a few hundred years this custom became binding. Today one of the most basic Rabbinic laws is that a man may not walk four cubits

1000 prophets, one is required to obey the teaching of the 1001 rabbis. See further Appendix 3.

[19] *Chidushei Ramban*, Pesachim 7b [Or Olam ed. p. 8a]; *Beit Yoseph*, Orach Chayim 128:6 [vol. 1 p. 111b]; *Mishnah Berurah* 125:8 [vol. 1 p. 300].

[20] The Talmud reports matter-of-factly:

> "Men sometimes cover their heads and sometimes not; but women's hair is always covered, and children are always bareheaded." (*Babylonian Talmud*, Nedarim 30b)

without his head covered nor make a blessing (even while seated) without his head covered.[21] Sanctified customs such as these are in direct violation of the Torah which commands us:

> You shall not add unto the matter which I command you today nor shall you diminish aught from it, to keep the commandments of YHWH your God which I am commanding you. (Deuteronomy 4:2)

The same principle is repeated in Deuteronomy 12:32 [Hebrew: 13:1],

> All that I am commanding you, you shall diligently do; you shall not add to it or diminish from it.

We are also taught in the book of Proverbs,

> Do not add unto His words, lest He reprove you and you be found a liar. (Proverbs 30:6)

Making customs into law, no matter how ancient the custom, is a violation of the Torah and makes those that do so into liars.

Iniquity #5: Man-Made Laws

The fifth iniquity of the Rabbis is the outright enactment of new laws. These invented Rabbinic laws are called *takanot* תַּקָּנוֹת ("enactments, reforms") or *mitzvot derabanan* מִצְוֹת דְּרַבָּנָן ("commandments of our Rabbis").[22] The classic example of a *takanah* – "enactment, reform" – (singular of *takanot*) is the washing of the hands which is a law enacted by the Rabbis. Because the Rabbis enacted this law, and because God supposedly commanded us to obey the Rabbis (at least according to the Oral

[21] *Shulchan Aruch*, Orach Hayyim 2:6 [vol. 1 pp. 11–12]; *Bi'ur Halachah*, 91 [vol. 1 p. 248].

[22] The opposite of *mitzvot derabanan* מִצְוֹת דְּרַבָּנָן "Commandments of Our Rabbis" are *mitzvot de'orayta* מִצְוֹת דְּאוֹרָיְיתָא "Commandments of the Torah"! The opposite of *takanah* "(Rabbinical) Enactment" is *halachah* הֲלָכָה "(Biblical) Law."

Law), the blessing can be made: "Blessed art thou Lord, King of the universe, who has sanctified us with his commandments **and commanded us** to wash the hands."

As I explained these five iniquities of the Rabbis to my Torah-keeping Christian friend, I began to realize that what was second nature to me was completely alien to someone uninitiated in Rabbinical/Pharisaic Judaism. I now understood what a precarious position my friend was in. As a "Torah-keeping Christian" he was attempting to understand Yeshua's message spoken to Judean and Galilean Israelites 2000 years ago. But my friend was missing the whole point of Yeshua's message because he had not known about the "Five Iniquities" which the Rabbis were trying to impose on the Israelite population of ancient Judah and Galilee. When he read that Yeshua did away with the traditions of the elders to wash the hands he thought this was an annulment of Torah. But to me it was obvious that Yeshua was speaking out against the man-made laws of the Pharisees and actually upholding Torah. This is what he meant when he said, "Why do ye also transgress the commandment of God by your tradition?" You violate Deuteronomy 4:2 and 12:32 [13:1] by adding to the Torah.

Yeshua continues, "Thus have ye made the commandment of God of none effect by your tradition." (Matthew 15:6 [KJV]). By keeping the nation busy with their man-made laws, the Rabbis were distancing people from the Torah. This is a message that rings as true today as it did 2000 years ago. In modern Israel about 70% of the Jews are "secularist" which means they do not live by Torah. If you ask the average Israeli why he has shut Torah out of his life, he will generally tell you that being "religious" is too difficult and its not what God wants anyway. When you ask for an example, he'll cite you a thousand and one things the Rabbis require, which have no basis in the Torah. Now these secularists are not stupid. They know these Rabbinical laws are not from the Torah but they usually do not realize that there is a way to live by Torah without being sucked in by Rabbinical innovations. So they end up throwing out the baby with the bath water. In essence, by requiring these man-made laws, the Rabbis are driving people away from Torah.

Chapter 4
Was Yeshua a Karaite?

As I was sitting and conversing with my Torah-keeping Christian friend, I began to realize that Yeshua's message had a Karaite streak to it. He was speaking out against the man-made laws of the Rabbis to bring people back to the Torah which is the primary message of Karaite Judaism. As my friend continued reading to me from Matthew 15 my suspicions about Yeshua seemed to be confirmed. After criticizing the Pharisees for making the Torah of no effect by their man-made traditions, Yeshua then quoted Isaiah 29:13,

> (7) Ye hypocrites, well did Esaias prophesy of you, saying, (8) This people draweth nigh unto me with their mouth, and honoureth me with their lips; but their heart is far from me. (9) But in vain they do worship me, **<u>teaching for doctrines the commandments of men</u>**. (Matthew 15:7–9 [KJV])

The expression "teaching for doctrines the commandments of men" is a paraphrase of Isaiah 29:13. Isaiah actually speaks about *mitzvat anashim melumada* מִצְוַת אֲנָשִׁים מְלֻמָּדָה "a learned commandment of men,"[23] that is a man-made law which has become habit by doing it over and over. When I read that Yeshua criticized the man-made commandments of the Rabbis basing his words on Isaiah 29:13, I was both impressed and surprised. In the Middle Ages, Isaiah 29:13 became the battle cry of the Karaites against Rabbanite innovations and this phrase appears countless times in medieval Karaite writings.[24] But here was Yeshua saying the same thing hundreds of years earlier. He seemed to me to be a 1st Century Karaite.

Who Are the Karaites?

I asked my friend what he thought of this. At first he was quite offended. He knew I was a Karaite but thought that Karaism was a "sect" that had only been invented in the Middle Ages. So how could Yeshua be a Karaite?! My friend had even read the age-old Rabbinical tale about Anan Ben David whom the Rabbis claim founded Karaism because he was upset after being spurned by the Rabbis. When I heard this I could not suppress a chuckle. The Rabbis tell this story about all their enemies. According to the Talmud, Yeshua founded Christianity because he was spurned by his teacher Rabbi Joshua ben Perahjah;[25] according to another

[23] Others translate Isaiah 29:13: "taught by the precept of men" (KJV); "taught by the commandment of men" (NKJV); "commandment of men learned by rote" (JPS, RSV); "tradition learned by rote" (NASB); "rules taught by men" (NIV).

[24] For example, the 9th Century Karaite sage Daniel al-Kumisi writes in his *Epistle to the Dispersion* (Nemoy ed. p. 88): "Abandon the learned commandments of men that are not from the Torah; do not accept anything from anyone except that which is written in the Torah of the Lord alone." The biblical phrase "learned commandment of men" *mitzvat anashim melumada* מִצְוַת אֲנָשִׁים מְלֻמָּדָה appears no less than twelve times in Kumisi's 12-page *Epistle to the Dispersion*!

[25] The Talmudic story about Yeshua appears in the following Talmudic passage:

> What of R. Joshua b. Perahjah?... One day he (R. Joshua) was reciting the Shema', when Jesus came before him. He intended to receive him and made a sign to him. He (Jesus) thinking that it was to repel him, went, put up a brick, and worshipped it. 'Repent,' said he (R. Joshua) to him. He replied, 'I have thus learned from thee: He who sins and causes

Rabbinic legend Mohammed founded Islam because he was spurned by the Jews of Mecca. I explained this to my friend and he admitted that it did not seem very plausible that someone would teach people to obey Torah just to get revenge on the Rabbis. My friend wanted to know more. Who was this Anan fellow anyway? I explained that Anan was not even a Karaite. In fact, the Karaites of his period scorned Anan, for although he rejected Rabbinical authority, he still held on to the irrational methods of interpretations employed by the Rabbis. Because of this his followers were rejected by the Karaites and labeled "Ananites."[26]

My friend was by now quite confused. If Karaites were not invented by Anan then where did they come from? I reminded him what I had explained earlier about the Talmud being written down in 500 CE in Babylonia. Once the Talmud was written down it was no longer the secret knowledge of a handful of rabbis. As a result, Talmudism began to spread across the Jewish world. As more and more Jews began to identify themselves as Talmudic, other Jews protested that *their* ancestors had known nothing of this Oral Law but only obeyed the Hebrew Scriptures (="Old Testament").[27] In those days the Hebrew Scriptures were called

others to sin is not afforded the means of repentance.' And a Master has said, 'Jesus the Nazarene practised magic and led Israel astray.' (*Babylonian Talmud*, Sanhedrin 107b (uncensored version) [Soncino Translation])

[26] See Kirkisani pp. 103, 146–147. The Karaite attitude towards Anan is epitomized by the fact that his own followers called him *rosh hamaskilim* רֹאשׁ הַמַּשְׂכִּילִים "Head of the Enlightened" while the Karaites mockingly called him *rosh haksilim* רֹאשׁ הַכְּסִילִים "Head of the Fools" (Kirkisani pp. 94–95).

[27] Anan's was a sort of Martin Luther King of his day. Shortly after the Talmud began to spread to new areas where it was previously unknown, the Islamic Empire burst forth on history bringing most Jews under Islamic rule. As Talmudism met increasing resistance, the Rabbis began to use the Islamic sword to impose their new doctrine. In many areas this led to great persecution and violence. Anan's great accomplishment was that (like the great civil rights leader Martin Luther King) he

"Kara" קְרָא[28] and those Jews who insisted on exclusive loyalty to the Hebrew Scriptures became known as "Karaites" קָרָאִים.[29] I explained to my friend that in earlier times it was a given that all Israelites would follow Scripture so there was no reason to label one segment of the population as Karaite or "Scripturalist." Everyone was a Scripturalist, at least all those who could control themselves long enough not to bow down to Baal or sacrifice to *'Ashtoret* (Easter). In this sense Moses was a Karaite, that is, a Scripturalist, from the moment the Torah was given. So were Isaiah and Jeremiah, and all the prophets of Israel. They were all Karaites because all of them believed in the truth of the Hebrew Scriptures while rejecting man-made laws and false revelations (Deuteronomy 4:2; Isaiah 29:13; Jeremiah 16:19). After I explained this, my friend began to understand what I meant when I said Yeshua sounded like a 1st Century Karaite. Like Isaiah and Jeremiah, Yeshua taught people to return to Torah while at the same time he told them to leave off the man-made laws. This aspect of his message was Karaite, even if in those days no one used this word yet.

My friend asked me if I could think of another example in history of a movement existing long before it was given a name. Naturally what came to mind was the "*Misnagdim*," the dominant movement in Rabbinical Judaism in 18th Century Lithuania, of which my own ancestors were leaders. In those days the Rabbis were divided into two camps, the *Hasidim* or "righteous" who followed the new form of Rabbanism invented by the *Ba'al Shem-Tov*, and the *Misnagdim* or "opponents" who opposed the new

used non-violent resistance to convince the Muslim authorities to allow non-Talmudists to continue practicing their ancient observance of Torah.

28 The name *Kara* for the Hebrew Scriptures has survived in Modern Hebrew in the form *Mikra* מִקְרָא. The more commonly used "Tanach" is an acronym which only came into use in the last 500 years.

29 See Ben Yehudah vol. 12 pp. 6138–6139 nt. 3.

ways of the *Hasidim*. The *Hasidim* gave absolute authority to a single rabbi whom they dubbed "The *Rebbe*" and spent most of their time engaged in so-called mystical pursuits.[30] In contrast, the *Misnagdim* gave different amounts of authority to different rabbis based on their Talmudic knowledge and spent most of their time studying Talmud and other legal texts. Any rabbi could attain high standing among the *Misnagdim* based on his scholarly achievements while a *Hasidic* "Rebbe" had to either perform miracles or inherit his position from his father. To this very day Jews of Lithuanian extraction proudly proclaim that they are *Misnagdim* ("Opponents") who preserve the original Rabbinical Judaism. In this sense the *Misnagdim* would claim that Rabbi Akiva was a *Misnaged* (singular of *Misnagdim*) even though he lived 1600 years before the *Misnagdim* movement got its name. But there is no doubt the *Misnagdim* are right! Rabbi Akiva – who lived 1600 years before the *Ba'al Shem-Tov* – was not a *Hasid*; he did not believe in a single Rabbinical leader who performed miracles (remember the miracles of Rabbi Eliezer!). There can be no doubt that the *Misnagdim* ("Opponents") are the preservers of an earlier form of Rabbanism which existed for centuries before they received the name *Misnagdim*, while the *Hasidim* ("Righteous") were those who invented an entirely new religious doctrine.

30 Perhaps the best-known example of *Hasidim* are the Lubavitch who follow Rabbi Schneerson.

Chapter 5
A Contradiction in Greek Matthew?

After the conversation with my Torah-keeping Christian friend I did not give much more thought to the Karaite aspect of Yeshua's message. After all, I had read the New Testament and knew there were other aspects of Yeshua's message which seemed decidedly un-Karaite (see chapter 10 below). Then I was approached with the question about Matthew 23:1–3. The textual problem was quite clear. In Matthew 15 Yeshua seems to be telling his disciples to stay away from the man-made commandments of the Pharisees while in Mathew 23:1–3 he was telling them to obey whatever the Pharisees teach because they sit in the seat of Moses and have his authority.

As a Karaite, my first reaction was still that I was not too concerned at what appeared to be a contradiction between Matthew 15 and Matthew 23. Yet I decided I would approach this as a textual problem, in the same way that I might try and figure out a textual difficulty in the Dead Sea Scrolls or other ancient writings.

One of the first "solutions" I came across was from a so-called Bible Critic, one of those learned professors sitting in their ivory towers. The view from the ivory tower was that Matthew 15 was written by an anti-Pharisee disciple of Yeshua while Matthew 23 was written by a pro-Pharisee disciple. Each of these disciples simply heard in Yeshua's words what he wanted to hear based on his own preconceived notions.[31] I did not rule this explanation out but was not too impressed by it either. It seemed to be quite a bit of speculation to assume that there was a split like this among the early followers of Yeshua. Were there really pro-Pharisaic and anti-Pharisaic factions in the "early Church"? Maybe, but I had yet to see a single historical reference to this effect.[32] Surely this would have left other traces in the historical and textual record.

Most Christian scholars simply admitted that Yeshua could not have meant for his disciples to obey the Pharisees but were unable to offer any plausible explanation of the fact that the book of Matthew attributes these words to him.[33] For some time, I had no solution to this problem and was not really sure how to proceed. I tried checking Matthew 23:2–3 in the "original" Greek. As a Karaite my approach to the Tanach has always been to read it in the original Hebrew since every translation contains an *implicit* interpretation. Actually, this is my approach to any ancient document. If I want to know what the Talmud says I read it in

[31] For example, Fenton p. 366: "It is difficult to believe Jesus really commanded obedience to the teaching of the scribes and Pharisees; this seems to have been the attitude of Matthew or one of his sources; see 5[19]." Compare also Davies and Allison p. 269.

[32] One possible exception is Acts 15:5. This passage may refer to the desire of a Pharisaic faction among Yeshua's followers to impose Pharisaic laws and traditions upon all "believers." This was opposed by James (Ya'akov) who instead recommends four basic laws to start off new believers and explains that the rest of the commandments can be ascertained by simply hearing the Torah of Moses read in the synagogue every Sabbath (Acts 15:20–21). Of course, anyone learning the commandments by hearing the Torah read would not be subjected to the man-made laws of the Pharisees which are absent from the written Torah.

[33] See for example, Davies and Allison p. 270.

Aramaic and if I want to know what the Dead Sea Scrolls say, I read them in Hebrew. So I checked the Greek of Matthew 23:2–3 and found that the standard English translations had faithfully represented what was written in the Greek.

Chapter 6
Greek or Hebrew?

After finding that Matthew 23:2–3 said the same thing in the Greek as in the English, I was pretty much out of ideas. My field of study was really Tanach, Dead Sea Scrolls, and ancient Judaism. Although I studied Greek at the university, New Testament studies were not really my field of expertise. So I asked a few of my colleagues at the university if they could give me a clue as to where to go next. One of my colleagues told me that some scholars were of the opinion that parts of the first three Gospels of the New Testament were originally written in Hebrew. I asked why they thought this. He answered, "Because they are full of Hebraisms."

I knew all about Hebraisms from my study of the Septuagint, the ancient Greek translation of the Tanach. World-renowned experts in classical Greek find the Septuagint incomprehensible while any Israeli student can read it after only a couple of years of learning Greek. The reason is that the Septuagint was translated by very bad translators. Rather than translate the Tanach into proper Greek, they mechanically translated the words, leaving behind numerous Hebrew thought patterns. To someone who is familiar with the Tanach in Hebrew this Greek is relatively easy to read. But to a Classical Greek specialist who expects to find elegant Greek syntax it sounds like gibberish. And in ancient times it was no better. As one of my professors says, "On the streets of Athens they did not understand the Septuagint." To the ancient Greek reader this translation was incomprehensible. For example, the Tanach often opens an account with the Hebrew word *vayehi* וַיְהִי "and it was." Of course in Hebrew "and it was" means, "it came to pass, it happened." But the Greek reader sees *kai egeneto* καὶ ἐγένετο and says, And it was? And *what* was?! In Greek its gibberish! Very often the translators did not even know what they were reading and created nonsensical sentences by translating word for word.[34] This is like what happened to a friend of mine at Hebrew University who wrote a paper in English and then hired someone to translate it into Hebrew. At one point in the paper my friend referred to a graph with the words: "See Table 1." The Israeli translator, having only a basic working knowledge of English, translated this *re'e shulchan 'echad* רְאֵה שׁוּלְחָן אֶחָד "see the one table you eat on." Of course, the Hebrew word *shulchan* means a table you eat on not a table in a document which in Hebrew is a different word altogether (*tavla* טַבְלָה)! When my friend read this translation he did not know whether to laugh or cry. This is the type of translation one often finds in the Septuagint, an over-literalized translation by someone who is not entirely sure what he is translating. To complicate matters, numerous Greek copyists who did not know any Hebrew tried to "improve" what was clearly

[34] For example, in the Septuagint see LXX 1 Samuel 3:10 (compare LXX Numbers 24:1). Some interesting examples in the Greek Matthew are discussed by Grintz pp. 36–39. As one grammar of New Testament Greek puts it, "Major Semitisms... are not only bad Greek but are apt to cause difficulty in translation..." (Whittaker p. 150).

poor Greek. The result was a translation which at times mimics the Hebrew word for word and at other times wildly differs from it.

After a quick perusal of the first three gospels in Greek I could see they contained some Hebraisms. Certainly not to the same extent as the Septuagint, but they were there. Blass and Debrunner, the standard grammar of New Testament Greek, explains the situation:

> Many expressions which a Greek would not have used were bound to creep into a faithful written translation of a Semitic original.[35]

Blass and Debrunner go on to say that these Semitic expressions are "Aramaisms." After a little more research I discovered there was a long-standing debate among New Testament scholars about whether certain parts of the New Testament (especially Matthew, Mark, Luke, Acts, and Revelation) were originally written in Aramaic or Hebrew.[36] Those in favor of an Aramaic original were by far the majority, but as I gradually worked my way through the Greek of the first three Gospels I kept running into things like "and it was"[37] which could only be Hebraisms, not Aramaisms. In Aramaic this phrase is just as much gibberish as it is in Greek.

After a few grueling weeks immersed in New Testament Greek, I was no closer to an answer than when I had started. So what if the book of Matthew had been written in Hebrew or had Hebrew sources?! As fascinating as this was, how did this help me

35 Blass and Debrunner §4 p. 3. One grammar of New Testement Greek lists no less than twenty-three separate categories of Semitisms (Zerwick pp. 163–164).

36 For example, Lamsa argues that the entire New Testament was written in Aramaic while Grintz argues that Matthew was written in Hebrew. See Howard 1986a p. 223 for a survey of the two sides.

37 For example, *kai egeneto* καὶ ἐγένετο "and it was" appears at Matthew 7:28; Mark 1:9; Luke 1:23; etc.

understand Matthew 23:2–3? I went back to my colleague at the university and he confessed that he had left out the most important part. My colleague explained that not only did some scholars believe that Matthew was originally written in Hebrew, but a version of the Hebrew Matthew has survived to this day.

Chapter 7
Shem-Tov's Hebrew Matthew

When I heard that a Hebrew version of Matthew still existed, I immediately went to the Hebrew University library on Mt. Scopus and after a quick search on the computer found a book entitled *The Gospel of Matthew according to a Primitive Hebrew Text.* The author was George Howard, a competent scholar at an American university. I sat down and began to read his book which contained a Hebrew text of Matthew, an English translation of that text, and a linguistic and textual study. Before I went to the Hebrew text I decided to read through the linguistic and textual study to see what I was dealing with.

Howard explained that a Hebrew version of the book of Matthew had been preserved by a 14th Century Spanish Jew named Shem-Tov Ibn Shaprut. This Shem-Tov should not be confused with the *Ba'al Shem-Tov*, the Rabbinical "miracle worker" who founded *Hasidism* in the 18th Century; the Shem-Tov that preserved the Hebrew version of Matthew lived 400 years earlier. This 14th Century Shem-Tov lived in Spain during the Inquisition. This period was marked by the *Disputatio*, or in English,

"Disputations." These Disputations were public debates forced on the Jews by their Catholic oppressors. A Disputation might occur when a Catholic bishop sent his storm troopers into a nearby synagogue and dragged the local rabbi into the public square. The rabbi would then be forced to defend the Jewish faith on the spot. If the rabbi lost, the local Jewish population could be forcibly converted to Catholicism; if he won he could be charged with insulting the Catholic religion and be forced to flee for his life.[38] The Disputation was really a no-win situation but most Jews would agree that becoming a refugee is preferable to being forcibly converted to Catholicism.

Shem-Tov Ibn Shaprut lived at the height of these Disputations and to help his fellow Jews he sat down and wrote a polemical treatise refuting Catholicism. Shem-Tov's polemical approach was to go through the New Testament section by section searching for weaknesses that could be used against the Catholics. Interestingly enough, one of his common tactics was to point to verses where the Catholics violate the direct instructions of Yeshua.[39] At the end of Shem-Tov's polemical treatise, entitled *Even Bochan* ("Test Stone"), he included a Hebrew version of the book of Matthew as a sort of appendix. Shem-Tov explained that if his fellow Jews were to survive these Disputations they had better start reading the New Testament. The Hebrew version of Matthew appended to the end of Shem-Tov's *Even Bochan* is now generally referred to as "Shem-Tov's Hebrew Matthew."

[38] A good book on the Disputations is still Eisenstein's *Ozar Wikuhim* (see Bibliography). A good example of a Jew who was forced to flee after winning a Disputation is Nachmanides (1194–1270).

[39] For example, on Matthew 12:1–8, Shem-Tov points out that the Catholics have done away with the Sabbath even though Yeshua clearly upheld it. See also Garshowitz pp. 307–309.

Shem-Tov's Hebrew Matthew was known for centuries but it was always assumed that Shem-Tov simply translated his version of Matthew from Greek or Latin into Hebrew. Then in the 1980s George Howard of Mercer University in Georgia carried out a detailed linguistic study in which he showed that there were parts of Shem-Tov's Hebrew Matthew which could not be easily explained as translations from Greek. When I got to the part in Howard's book with the linguistic study I was excited; now I was back in my element.

One of the things Howard found in Shem-Tov's Hebrew Matthew was Hebrew word puns.[40] A *word pun* is a play on words that builds on similar sounding Hebrew roots used multiple times with different meanings. They are a common feature of the Tanach and form an integral part of Hebrew story-telling. For example, the first man is named *Adam* אָדָם because he is taken out of the earth which in Hebrew is *Adamah* אֲדָמָה. There is actually another Hebrew word for "earth" *'aretz* אָרֶץ, which could have been used in Genesis. But the word *Adamah* ("earth") is used repeatedly throughout Genesis 2 as a word pun which contrasts with *Adam*.

In another example the Torah tells us that the man and his wife were naked, in Hebrew *'arumim* עֲרוּמִּים (Genesis 2:25). The very next verse informs us that the snake was clever, in Hebrew *'arum* עָרוּם (Genesis 3:1). This is another word pun contrasting "naked" *'arumim* עֲרוּמִּים with "clever" *'arum* עָרוּם. This word pun provides no message whatsoever; it is simply part of the texture and style of Hebrew story-telling.

Another example can be found in one of Jeremiah's first visions:

> (11) And the word of YHWH came to me saying, What do you see Jeremiah? And I said, I see an almond (*shaked*

[40] For more details see Howard 1987 pp. 194–201 and Howard 1995 pp. 184–190.

> שָׁקֵד) branch. (12) And YHWH said to me, you have seen well, for I am diligent (*shoked* שֹׁקֵד) to do my word. (Jeremiah 1:11–12)

Here the word pun is interwoven into Jeremiah's vision. He sees an almond branch, in Hebrew *shaked* שָׁקֵד, as a sign that YHWH is diligent, in Hebrew *shoked* שֹׁקֵד. Of course, in English this whole passage makes no sense. Whereas the Hebrew connection is obvious, the English reader is left wondering how an almond branch relates to the Creator diligently doing his word.

Word puns such as these are extremely common and can be found on nearly every page of the Hebrew Scriptures. It was surprising however when Howard found Hebrew word puns in Shem-Tov's Hebrew Matthew because it was supposed to be a translation from the Greek.

For example, in Hebrew Matthew 18:9 Yeshua says, "If your eye causes you to stumble (*tachshilcha* תַּכְשִׁילְךָ)… cast it from you (*tashlicheha* תַּשְׁלִיכֶהָ)."[41] This contains a word pun between the similar sounding words *tachshilcha* "causes you to stumble" and *tashlicheha* "cast it from you." *How did Hebrew word puns get into a book translated from Greek?*

Of course, one word pun is hardly evidence that a book was written in Hebrew since this could just be a coincidence. It's when they start multiplying that they become difficult to explain as translations from a Greek original. But there seem to be quite a few Hebrew word puns in Shem-Tov's Hebrew Matthew. For example, "And the crowds saw (*vayir'u* וַיִּרְאוּ) and they feared (*vayir'u* וַיִּרְאוּ) very much" (Hebrew Matthew 9:8[42]). In this

[41] Matthew 18:9 in Shem-Tov's Hebrew Matthew:

וְאִם עֵינֶיךָ [צ״ל: עֵינְךָ] **תַּכְשִׁילְךָ**. . . **וְתַשְׁלִיכֶהָ** מִמֶּךָּ

All Shem-Tov's Hebrew Matthew texts have been adapted from Howard's editions unless otherwise noted. Vowels were added by myself.

[42] Matthew 9:8 in Shem-Tov's Hebrew Matthew:

וַיִּרְאוּ [=**רָאוּ**] הַחֲבוּרוֹת **וַיִּרְאוּ** [=**יָרְאוּ**] מְאֹד

example, homonyms derived from two different roots (*r'h* ר.א.ה. "to see" vs. *yr'* י.ר.א. "to fear") are juxtaposed as a word pun. A more complex example can be found in Matthew 12:13, 15:

> (13) Then he said to the man, stretch out your hand, and he stretched out (*vayet* **וַיֵּט**) his hand… (15) And it was after this that Yeshua knew and he turned from there (*vayet* **וַיֵּט**) and many sick people went after him…[43]

Here the word *vayet* **וַיֵּט** is used twice with two different meanings ("and he stretched out"; "and he turned") in close proximity. A similar example can be found in Matthew 14:35–36:

> (35) …and they brought him everyone who was sick (*ha-cholim* **הַחוֹלִים**) with all types of illnesses. (36) And they entreated (*ve-chilu* **וְחִלּוּ**) him…[44]

In this example, the root *chlh* ח.ל.ה. is used with two distinct meanings ("sick", "entreated"), a typical Hebrew word pun.

There are even examples where a word pun is interwoven into an entire passage. For example, in Matthew 18:23 Yeshua begins a parable which uses the verb *shalem* **שַׁלֵּם** "to pay" five times. He then concludes in v.35, "So shall my father in heaven do if you do not forgive each man his brother with a complete (*shalem* **שָׁלֵם**) heart."[45] The moral of the parable uses the same

[43] Matthew 12:13, 15 in Shem-Tov's Hebrew Matthew:
(13) אָז אָמַר לָאִישׁ נְטֵה יָדְךָ, **וַיֵּט** יָדוֹ. . . (15) וַיְהִי אַחֲרֵי זֹאת וַיֵּדַע יֵשׁוּ[עַ] **וַיֵּט** מִשָּׁם וַיֵּלְכוּ אַחֲרָיו חוֹלִים רַבִּים. . .

[44] Matthew 14:35—36 in Shem-Tov's Hebrew Matthew:
(35) . . .וְהֵבִיאוּ לוֹ כֹּל **הַחוֹלִים** מִכֹּל מַדְוִים. (36) **וְחִלּוּ** פָּנָיו. . .

[45] Matthew 18:23—35 in Shem-Tov's Hebrew Matthew:
(23) בָּעֵת הַהִיא אָמַר יֵשׁוּ[עַ] לְתַלְמִידָיו, מַלְכוּת שָׁמַיִם דוֹמֶה הִיא לְאָדָם מֶלֶךְ יוֹשֵׁב לַעֲשׂוֹת חֶשְׁבּוֹן עִם עֲבָדָיו וּמְשָׁרְתָיו: (24) וְכַאֲשֶׁר הִתְחִיל לַחֲשׁוֹב בָּא אֶ[חָד] שֶׁהוּא חַיָּיב כַּעֲשֶׂרֶת אֲלָפִים זְהוּבִים: (25) וְאֵין לוֹ מַה לִיתֵּן וַיְצַו אֲדוֹנָיו לִמְכּוֹר אוֹתוֹ וְאֶת בָּנָיו וְאֶת כָּל אֲשֶׁר לוֹ **לְשַׁלֵּם** הַמָּמוֹן: (26) וַיִּפּוֹל הָעֶבֶד לִפְנֵי אֲדוֹנָיו וַיִּתְחַנֵּן לוֹ לְרַחֵם עָלָיו וּלְהַמְתִּין לוֹ כִּי הַכֹּל **יְשַׁלֵּם** [אוֹ: **יְשַׁלֵּם**]: (27) וַיַּחְמוֹל עָלָיו אֲדוֹנָיו וּמָחַל לוֹ הַכֹּל: (28) וַיֵּצֵא הָעֶבֶד הַהוּא וַיִּמְצָא אֶחָד מֵחֲבֵירָיו שֶׁהוּא חַיָּיב לוֹ מֵאָה מָעוֹת וַיַּחֲזֵק בּוֹ, וַיִּפְגַּע לוֹ [חֲבֵרוֹ] לֵאמֹר: (29) חוּסָה עָלַי וְהַמְתֵּן לִי וְהַכֹּל

exact root *shalem* ש.ל.ם. with a different meaning ("complete" vs. "pay"), another typical word pun.

One of the main proofs cited by those who believe that Matthew was written in Greek is actually a word pun in the Greek itself. In Matthew 16:18 Yeshua says to Simeon, "…You are Peter (*Petros* Πέτρος), and upon this rock (*petrai* πέτρᾳ) I will build my church…" (Matthew 16:18). This word pun is based on the Greek word *petra* meaning "rock" from which Peter's name (*Petros*) is derived.[46] This is usually brought as a decisive proof for a Greek Matthew original since it is clear that the Greek word pun is interwoven with the content of the passage. But in the Hebrew there is a different word pun not found in the Greek! In Hebrew Matthew 16:18 Yeshua says, "…You are a stone (*'even* **אֶבֶן**) and I will build (*'evneh* **אֶבְנֶה**) my house of prayer upon you." In Hebrew, the word pun is between *'even* **אֶבֶן** "stone" and the verb *'evneh* **אֶבְנֶה** "I will build."[47] This word pun is significant because it is based on a similar word pun in Psalms 118:22 "The stone (*'even* **אֶבֶן**) that the builders (*bonim* **בּוֹנִים**) refused, has become the chief cornerstone" which is later quoted in Matthew 21:42, 44![48]

Why are all these word puns important? If Shem-Tov's Hebrew Matthew was a translation from Greek, then where did these word puns come from? The purpose of a word pun is to beautify the text. But why would a 14th Century Rabbi writing a

אֲשַׁלֵּם: (30) וְלֹא אָבָה לִשְׁמוֹעַ לוֹ וַיּוֹלִיכוּהוּ לְבֵית הַסּוֹהַר עַד **שַׁלֵּם** לוֹ הַכֹּל: (31) וְרָאוּ עַבְדֵי הַמֶּלֶךְ אֵת אֲשֶׁר עָשָׂה וַיִּחַר לָהֶם מְאֹד וַיָּבֹאוּ וַיַּגִּידוּ לַאֲדוֹנֵיהֶם: (32) אָז קָרָא אוֹתוֹ אֲדוֹנָיו וַיֹּאמֶר לוֹ, עֶבֶד אָרוּר! הֲלֹא מָחַלְתִּי לְךָ כֹּל חוֹבֶיךָ כַּאֲשֶׁר פִּיַּיסְתָּנִי? (33) וּמַדּוּעַ לֹא מָחַלְתָּ לְעַבְדְּךָ בְּהִתְחַנְּנוֹ אֵלֶיךָ כַּאֲשֶׁר מְחַלְתִּיךָ? (34) וַיִּחַר אַף אֲדוֹנָיו בּוֹ וַיְצַו לְעַנּוֹתוֹ עַד **יְשַׁלֵּם** לוֹ כֹּל הַחוֹב: (35) כֵּן יַעֲשֶׂה לָכֶם אָבִי שֶׁבַּשָּׁמַיִם אִם לֹא תִּמְחֲלוּ אִישׁ אֶת אָחִיו בְּלֵב **שָׁלֵם**:

[46] This type of word pun is also called a "name explanation."

[47] Matthew 16:18 in Shem-Tov's Hebrew Matthew:

וַאֲנִי אוֹמֵר לְךָ שֶׁאַתָּה **אֶבֶן** וַאֲנִי **אֶבְנֶה** עָלֶיךָ בֵּית תְּפִלָּתִי. . .

[48] Compare Howard 1995 p. 185.

book to refute Catholic Christianity bother to beautify a Hebrew translation of Matthew?

There is other evidence besides word puns which seem to support a Hebrew original. In some instances it seems as if the Greek Matthew does not make sense or presents a difficult reading while Shem-Tov's Hebrew Matthew makes perfect sense. For example, in Greek it says, "For all the prophets and the law prophesied **until** John." (Matthew 11:13 [KJV]).[49] If I were Shem-Tov writing a polemic against Catholic Christianity I would have brought this verse as my first argument. Here in black and white the Greek Matthew says that the Tanach was not talking about Yeshua; the Tanach only prophesied up until John the Baptist while Yeshua's ministry was not foretold by the Tanach. That's what it says in the Greek Matthew! The Hebrew Matthew, though, has a slight but highly significant change. The Hebrew says, "For all the prophets and the Torah spoke **concerning** John" (Hebrew Matthew 11:13).[50] This Hebrew text makes more sense. The Hebrew is saying that throughout the Tanach there are references to a prophet such as John the Baptist (perhaps one can point to Malachi's final prophecy as an example). In Greek, the words for "until" and "concerning" are substantially different (*heos* ἕως vs. *peri* περὶ) but in Hebrew the difference is only one single letter (*'ad* עַד vs. *'al* עַל).[51] So, if Shem-Tov's Hebrew Matthew were just a translation from Greek, then the Greek text on which it was based had a substantially different reading from the Greek Matthew known today. But if the Greek Matthew is a

[49] Matthew 11:13 in Greek: πάντες γὰρ οἱ προφῆται καὶ ὁ νόμος **ἕως** Ἰωάννου ἐπροφήτευσαν

[50] Matthew 11:13 in Shem-Tov's Hebrew Matthew:

שֶׁכָּל הַנְּבִיאִים וְהַתּוֹרָה דִּבְּרוּ **עַל** יוֹחָנָן

[51] The parallel in Luke 16:16 also reads "until John" but using a different Greek word for "until" *mechri* μέχρι.

translation from Hebrew, then the Hebrew original it was based on was very similar to Shem-Tov's Hebrew Matthew.[52]

	Greek Matthew "until"	Hebrew Matthew "concerning"
Hebrew Equivalent	*'ad* עַד	*'al* עַל
Greek Equivalent	*heos* ἕως	*peri* περὶ

If Shem-Tov's Hebrew Matthew is just a translation from Greek, why would the Hebrew translation make more sense than the Greek original? It would have been in Shem-Tov's interest to preserve this Greek reading which lays the groundwork for a solid argument against Catholicism, which, after all, was his stated goal.[53]

If Shem-Tov's Hebrew Matthew is not a translation from Greek, then what is it? In the conclusion to his book, Howard explains:

> An investigation into this text leads to the conclusion that an old substratum to the Hebrew Matthew in Shem-Tob is a prior composition, not a translation. The old substratum, however, has been exposed to a series of revisions so that the present text of Shem-Tob represents the original only in an impure form.[54]

[52] Note that in the first edition of his book, Howard sees the Hebrew and Greek not as source and translation but as two "editions" of a single work (Howard 1987 p. 225). The line of reasoning presented here is my own. But compare Howard 1986a p. 225.

[53] Compare for example Shem-Tov's note on Matthew 21:5 which he points out contains a misquotation of Zechariah 9:9. Shem-Tov notes that Zechariah speaks about a female donkey whereas Matthew replaces this with a male donkey! Compare Howard 1987 p. 179.

[54] Howard 1987 p. 223. In the 1987 edition of his book Howard speaks about the original Hebrew Matthew as a first recension which may even predate the Greek

What this means is that Shem-Tov's Hebrew Matthew is not the "original" Matthew. But it may have original elements left behind from the original Matthew. To understand this more thoroughly one need only read through the actual Hebrew text of Matthew. After about ten chapters immersed in the Hebrew it is blatantly clear. Shem-Tov's Hebrew Matthew has been very clearly infected by the Greek Matthew to the point where it even contains Greek words transliterated into Hebrew. It seems as if someone sat down with the Hebrew Matthew in one hand and the Greek in the other and "corrected" the Hebrew according to the Greek. What apparently happened is throughout the ages people who were well-versed in the Greek text saw this Hebrew text of Matthew and thought it had "mistakes" in it. These mistakes or differences were actually in the Greek while the Hebrew had the original pure text written by Matthew himself. But these people versed in the Greek Matthew failed to realize this so they inadvertently "corrected" the Hebrew based on the Greek. So when Shem-Tov's Hebrew Matthew is identical to our modern Greek text, we can learn nothing new; it could just be a "correction" from the Greek. But when Shem-Tov's Hebrew Matthew differs from the Greek text it *may* contain "original readings" which were lost in the Greek.[55]

(Howard 1987 pp. 223–226). In the 1995 edition of his book entitled, *Hebrew Gospel of Matthew*, Howard scales back this conclusion (Howard 1995 p. 190), although he still maintains that "the unique and archaic readings in this text go back to the early centuries of the Christian era" (Howard 1995 p. 212). Elsewhere in the same study he writes: "Shem-Tob's Matthew, as printed above, does not preserve the original in a pure form. It reflects contamination by Jewish scribes during the Middle Ages. Considerable parts of the original, however, appear to remain, including its unpolished style, ungrammatical constructions, and Aramaized forms" (Howard 1995 p. 178). This conclusion is scaled back even more in Howard 1999 par.7.

[55] See also the two studies by Shedinger.

Chapter 8
Moses' Seat

Armed with this new knowledge I finally opened to Matthew 23:2–3 in Shem-Tov's Hebrew Matthew to see what it said. As already mentioned, the King James Translation of the Greek reads:

> (2) The scribes and the Pharisees sit in Moses' seat: (3) All therefore whatsoever **<u>they</u>** bid you observe, that observe and do; but do not ye after their works: for they say, and do not. (Matthew 23:2–3 [KJV])

But when I went to look in the Hebrew text of Matthew I found something quite different:

> (2) עַל כִּסֵּא מֹשֶׁה יֵשְׁבוּ הַפִּירוּשִׁים וְהַחֲכָמִים׃ (3) וְעַתָּה כֹּל אֲשֶׁר יֹאמַר לָכֶם שִׁמְרוּ וַעֲשׂוּ וּבְתַקָּנוֹתֵיהֶם וּמַעֲשֵׂיהֶם אַל תַּעֲשׂוּ שֶׁהֵם אוֹמְרִים וְהֵם אֵינָם עוֹשִׂים׃[56]

[56] Adapted from Howard 1987 p. 112. The Shem-Tov text is without vowels. Vowels were added by myself.

> (2) Al ki-se Mo-she yesh-vu ha-pi-ru-shim ve-ha-cha-cha-mim. (3) Ve-a-ta, kol a-sher yo-mar la-chem shim-ru va-asu u-ve-ta-ka-no-te-hem u-ma-a-se-hem al ta-a-su she-hem om-rim ve-hem e-nam o-sim.

This translates into English:

> (2) The Pharisees and sages sit upon the seat of Moses. (3) Therefore, all that **he** says to you, diligently do, but according to **their** reforms (*takanot* תַּקָּנוֹת) and **their** precedents (*ma'asim* מַעֲשִׂים) do not do, because they talk but they do not do.

In the Hebrew Matthew, Yeshua is telling his disciples *not* to obey the Pharisees. If their claim to authority is that they sit in *Moses' Seat*, **then diligently do as Moses says!**

To understand what happened, we must compare the Hebrew with the Greek. In the Greek, the disciples were commanded to obey "all that **they** [the Pharisees] say," but in the Hebrew, Yeshua told his disciples to obey "all that **he** [Moses] says." These are two fundamentally different messages, but in Hebrew, this is a difference of only one single letter! In Hebrew, "he says" is *yomar* יאמר while "they say" is *yomru* יאמרו. The only difference between the two in an un-pointed Hebrew text is the addition of the extra *vav* ו in *yomru* יאמרו "they say." That this is the basis for a completely different message is amazing because *vav* ו is one of the smallest letters in the Hebrew alphabet, really just a single stroke! The addition of this tiny letter changes Yeshua's message from an instruction to obey Moses ("all that **he** says") to a commandment to obey the Pharisees ("all that **they** say"). In contrast, in Greek the difference between "he says" (*eipei* εἴπῃ) and "they say" (*eiposin* εἴπωσιν) is a much larger difference. This suggests that the Greek translator misread the Hebrew text as containing that extra *vav* ו. Maybe this Greek translator did not even understand who or what the Pharisees were all about?

After instructing his disciples to do as Moses says, Yeshua continues that they must not do according to the *takanot* תַּקָּנוֹת and *ma'asim* מַעֲשִׂים of the Pharisees.[57] These two Hebrew words, *takanot* and *ma'asim*, are loaded with meaning when talking about the Pharisees. We already saw the word *takanot* when we discussed the "five iniquities" of the Rabbis. In Pharisee jargon *takanot* means "enactments, reforms" and more specifically "reforms that change biblical law." The Rabbis themselves distinguish between biblical law and their own invented laws which they call *takanot,* "reforms." The Jastrow Dictionary, the standard lexicon for post-Tanach Hebrew,[58] gives the following example of how the word *takanot* is used:

[57] In Howard's translation of Matthew 23:3 he translates "(they) say" (Howard 1987 p. 113) even though the Hebrew text on the opposite page contains the reading *yomar* יאמר "he says" (Howard 1987 p. 112)! Howard uses parentheses to indicate that his English translation has diverged from his Hebrew text. Apparently this divergence is because the six manuscripts Howard designates ABDEFG read *yomru* יאמרו "they say" while the British Library manuscript (Add. 26964 Folio 205b) and Manuscript C (Oxford-Bodleian Library MS Opp. Add. 4°. 72 Folio 76b) read *yomar* יאמר "he says" (the ninth manuscript examined by Howard, designated "H," is not preserved in Matthew 23:3). However, Howard himself explains (Howard 1987 pp.x–xi) that the British Library manuscript and MS C are the most reliable because the other manuscripts have gone through more "assimilation" in the direction of the Greek text. This means that when we find differences between the British Library manuscript (and C) and the other manuscripts in which the other manuscripts agree with the Greek, there is a strong likelihood that the British Library manuscript represents a more authentic reading (compare Howard 1995 pp. 182–183). This is why Howard himself chose the British Library manuscript as the basis for his printed edition. Nichols (see note 63 below) found that: "The Old Latin Manuscript ff2 also reads the singular at this point [dixerit]." In my own investigation I discovered that the reading *yomar* יאמר "he says" is also preserved in two other manuscripts of Shem-Tov's Hebrew Matthew which neither Howard nor Nichols examined: MS Roma-Biblioteca Casanatense 3099 and MS Livorno-Talmud Tora 53.

[58] The Jastrow Dictionary is specifically a dictionary of Hebrew and Aramaic used in early Rabbinic texts which roughly parallels the Hebrew spoken in 1st Century CE Judea and Galilee.

> Do you call these halakhoth (legal decisions)? these are **reforms [*takanot*]** (changing the Biblical law).[59]

If Shem-Tov's text of Matthew is correct, then Yeshua was warning his disciples not to follow the *takanot* or man-made laws of the Rabbis. Of course, this is consistent with what Yeshua taught his disciples in Matthew 15:3ff., "Why do ye also transgress the commandment of God by your tradition?… ye made the commandment of God of none effect by your tradition." [KJV]. Like the Karaite sages of the Middle Ages, Yeshua accused the Pharisees of putting their own invented laws above the law of the Torah. Interestingly, in the Hebrew of Matthew 15:3 the word translated as "tradition" is also *takanot*, "reforms that change biblical law"![60] So in the Hebrew Matthew there is a consistent thread throughout the book. Yeshua is preaching against the *takanot*, the Pharisaic reforms that change biblical law.

In the Greek Matthew 15:8–9 Yeshua then accuses the Pharisees of "teaching for doctrines the commandments of men," supposedly a quote from Isaiah 29:13. However, this is not exactly what Isaiah says. Isaiah actually talks about "learned commandments of men." Incredibly, the Hebrew Matthew has the precise quote from Isaiah, word for word.

Greek Matthew 15:9	"teaching for doctrines the commandments of men"
Hebrew Matthew 15:9	"learned commandments of men"
Hebrew Isaiah 29:13	"learned commandments of men"

[59] Jastrow p. 1693 under entry תַּקָּנָה citing *Babylonian Talmud,* Baba Metsia 112b.

[60] Matthew 15:1–3, 7–9 in Shem-Tov's Hebrew Matthew:

(1) אָז בָּאוּ אֶל יֵשׁוּ[עַ] הַחֲכָמִים וְהַפְּרוּשִׁים וַיֹּאמְרוּ אֵלָיו, (2) לָמָּה עוֹבְרִים תַּלְמִידֶ[י]ךָ **תַּקָּנוֹת** הָרִאשׁוֹנוֹת שֶׁהֵם אֵינָם רוֹחֲצִים יְדֵיהֶם קוֹדֶם הָאֲכִילָה? (3) וַיֹּאמֶר לָהֶם יֵשׁוּ[עַ], וְלָמָּה אַתֶּם עוֹבְרִים מַאַמְרֵי הָאֵל בְּעַד **תַּקָּנוֹתֵיהֶם**? . . .(7) הוֹי חֲנֵפִים! הִנֵּה יְשַׁעְיָה נִיבָּא מִכֶּם וְאָמַר, (8) כֹּה אָמַר [יְ]ה[וָ]ה], **׳יַעַן כִּי נִגַּשׁ הָעָם הַזֶּה בְּפִיו וּבִשְׂפָתָיו כִּבְּדוּנִי וְלִבּוֹ רִחַק מִמֶּנִי, (9) וַתְּהִי יִרְאָתָם אֹתִי מִצְוַת אֲנָשִׁים מְלוּמָּדָה**:׳

This is very significant, because if Shem-Tov Ibn Shaprut were translating from Greek and caught the New Testament misquoting Isaiah, he would have wanted to preserve that misquotation as accurately as possible to use as ammunition in his debates with the Catholics. But, if Shem-Tov's Hebrew Matthew is really a translation from Greek, then why do its quotations of the Tanach match the original Hebrew word for word, when the Greek quotations are at best paraphrases?

When I saw the accurate quotation of Isaiah 29:13 I was intrigued. The Karaite sages also accused the Pharisees of following "learned commandments of men" and as I mentioned previously, this phrase appears repeatedly in medieval Karaite writings.

The other thing Yeshua is said to have warned his disciples about in the Hebrew Matthew is the *ma'asim* מַעֲשִׂים of the Pharisees. According to the Jastrow Dictionary[61] *ma'asim* are "precedents" or to be more precise, **acts or deeds that serve as precedents**. The concept of *ma'asim* is unique to Pharisaic Judaism. It is not surprising that the Greek translator of Matthew had no idea what it was referring to so he translated it literally as *erga* ἔργα "actions or works." But Yeshua was talking about the *ma'asim* of the Pharisees which is something very specific. When a Pharisee does not know the law in a particular situation he looks for a precedent from one of his teachers. The Pharisees reason that if one of their teachers did a certain act it must be what the Oral Law requires. This is called a *ma'aseh* מַעֲשֶׂה or in plural *ma'asim* "precedents." This concept is canonized in the Talmudic rule *ma'aseh rav* מַעֲשֶׂה רַב "precedent is a teacher" (*Babylonian Talmud,* Sabbath 21a). The Talmud cites numerous *ma'asim* from which practical laws are derived. For example, the Rabbis have a rule that it is permissible to use a ramp built by a Gentile on the

[61] Jastrow p. 820.

Sabbath if it was not built specifically for the Jew. This strange Rabbinic ruling is derived from the following precedent:

> A *ma'aseh* in which Rabban Gamaliel and the elders were traveling in a ship, when a gentile made a ramp on which to descend, and Rabban Gamaliel, and the elders descended by it. (*Babylonian Talmud, Sabbath* 122a)

The Rabbis assumed that Rabban Gamaliel and the elders could not have sinned and therefore the fact that they used a ramp built on the Sabbath proves this is a permissible act. Learning precedents from the actions of the Rabbis is a standard method used by the Rabbis to derive religious law. There is no need for biblical proof because Rabbinic precedent is even better.[62]

According to the Hebrew Matthew, Yeshua is warning his disciples not to look to the *ma'asim*, the precedents of the Rabbis, as the standard for proper behavior. Nor are they to follow the *takanot*, the invented laws of the Rabbis. Instead they are to listen to what Moses says, because after all the Rabbinic claim to

[62] An alternative explanation of *ma'asim* "works," first suggested to me by Avi Ben Mordechai, is based on the use of this word in the document 4QMMT from the Dead Sea Scrolls. In 4QMMT (4Q398 14–17 ii:3), the phrase *ma'asei hatorah* מַעֲשֵׂי הַתּוֹרָה "works of the law" refers to the application of the Torah as interpreted by the authors of this legal document which at times significantly differs from what the Torah actually says. Based on this explanation, Yeshua would be instructing his disciples to follow the Torah but warning them not to accept the Pharisaic interpretations of the Torah. While this explanation is intriguing it suffers from two limitations. First, Matthew 23:3 speaks about *ma'asehem* מַעֲשֵׂיהֶם "their works," that is, the works of the Pharisees, and not *ma'asei hatorah* מַעֲשֵׂי הַתּוֹרָה "the works of the law" which is the actual phrase that appears in 4QMMT. Second, the phrase "works of the law" in the sense of an application of Torah as interpreted by the Pharisees (or by anyone else) never appears anywhere in the vast early Pharisaic literature preserved in the Mishnah, Tamud, and Midrash. On the other hand, most of this Pharisaic literature was not written down before the 3rd Century CE while 4QMMT proves this phrase was used in 1st Century CE Hebrew, at least by whoever wrote 4QMMT. This suggestion remains a possibility.

authority is that they sit in Moses' seat.[63] This is reminiscent of the teaching concerning the coin with the picture of Caesar on it (Matthew 22:20–21). If it is Caesar's coin, give it to Caesar.[64] If it is Moses' seat, do what Moses says.

[63] Credit must be given to Ross K. Nichols who, as far as I can tell, was the first scholar to note the variant reading *yomar* יאמר "he says" in Shem-Tov's Hebrew Matthew 23:3. Nichols writes in a study published at http://www.ancientpaths.org/ that he made this discovery in 1995. However, Nichols makes no reference to the *plus* reading of "and their *takanot*," the relationship of this *plus* reading to Hebrew Matthew 15, or the meaning of *ma'asim* within a Pharisaic context. Of course, Nichols says nothing about the Karaite connection.

[64] "And he saith unto them, Whose is this image and superscription? They say unto him, Caesar's. Then saith he unto them, Render therefore unto Caesar the things which are Caesar's; and unto God the things that are God's." (Matthew 22:20–21 [KJV]). In both the Hebrew and Greek Matthew it says to "return" to Caesar that which is Caesar's! If it's Caesar's coin, then give it back to him.

Chapter 9
They Talk But They Do Not Do

The last few words of Matthew 23:3 present a particularly interesting problem:

> ...but according to their reforms (*takanot*) and their precedents (*ma'asim*) do not do, **because they talk but they do not do** (Hebrew Matthew 23:3)

What did Yeshua mean when he said "they do not do"? What do they not do? When I first read this in Hebrew it sounded like something was missing at the end of the verse. At the same time, something about this seemed familiar but I was not sure what it was. Over the next few weeks, I continued to mull over the words "because they talk but they do not do." Something was missing here but what? The answer came to me in an entirely unexpected way. As a Karaite I am often confronted with people who have no idea what Karaite Judaism is. One of the most common misconceptions is that Karaites only believe in the Torah, the five books of Moses, and worship on Mt. Gerizim. As I always explain to people, it is the Samaritans up on Mt. Gerizim, not the

Karaites. Karaites believe in the entire Hebrew Scriptures from Genesis to Malachi, or actually in Hebrew, from Genesis to Chronicles (because in the Hebrew book order, Malachi is in the middle of the Bible). Karaites also recognize Jerusalem as the place where YHWH has chosen to place his name forever (2 Kings 21:7). The Samaritans, by contrast, are descendants of Babylonian Gentiles forcibly settled in the northern part of Israel by the Assyrian kings who worship at a "high-place" on Mt. Gerizim.[65]

The story of the Samaritans is told in 2 Kings 17. When these Babylonian Gentiles first settled in Samaria they were stricken by a series of lion attacks. They asked the king of Assyria to send them a priest from the exiled Israelites to pay homage to the local god. This priest was of course one of those evil priests who had served at the high-places which was one of the great sins of the northern tribes ever since the time of Jeroboam (2 Kings 17:21–23). But at least this priest brought a copy of the Torah with him and began to teach the Samaritans about YHWH. In the end, the Samaritans worshipped YHWH while at the same time worshipping their foreign ancestral gods (2 Kings 17:28–32).

One day I received yet another e-mail from a person confusing the Karaites with the Samaritans; I receive a few of these every week. When I sat down to answer this e-mail I decided to refresh my memory by re-reading 2 Kings 17. As I read the biblical account of the Samaritans I came across a verse which was difficult to understand. This Tanach verse was a synopsis of the Samaritans:

[65] Just as the Assyrians exiled the Ten Northern Tribes to foreign lands, they also brought foreigners and settled them in Israel. The idea was that a group of people in a strange environment with no ties to the land were more likely to be loyal to the imperial government than natives who had deep roots and a history of independence on their land.

1. Until this very day they do according to their former ways,
2. they do not fear YHWH, <u>and they do not do</u>,
3. according to their statutes and their judgments,
4. according to the Torah and commandments that YHWH commanded the children of Jacob. (2 Kings 17:34)[66]

This is a literal translation of the verse as it appears in Hebrew and clearly it does not make sense. It sounds as if the book of Kings is criticizing the Samaritans for **not** doing "according to their statutes and their judgments" when in the beginning of the very same verse it criticizes them for doing according to their former ways. So what is going on here?

All the standard English translations simply glaze over this problem by roughly paraphrasing the verse.[67] But if we stick to what it says in Hebrew we end up with this strange phrase "they do not do" which doesn't seem to fit in the verse. As I read this I knew that Hebrew syntax, the way sentences are structured, is quite different from English syntax. Sometimes one must read the Hebrew verse out loud several times to get the meaning. Having done this, the Hebrew made perfect sense, but had to be translated into English by re-ordering the four clauses of the verse as follows:[68]

[66] 2 Kings 17:34 in Hebrew:

1. עַד הַיּוֹם הַזֶּה הֵם עֹשִׂים כַּמִּשְׁפָּטִים הָרִאשֹׁנִים
2. אֵינָם יְרֵאִים אֶת יְהוָה וְאֵינָם עֹשִׂים
3. כְּחֻקֹּתָם וּכְמִשְׁפָּטָם
4. וְכַתּוֹרָה וְכַמִּצְוָה אֲשֶׁר צִוָּה יְהוָה אֶת בְּנֵי יַעֲקֹב אֲשֶׁר שָׂם שְׁמוֹ יִשְׂרָאֵל׃

[67] Most translations do this by omitting the word "their" which appears twice in the third clause in Hebrew.

[68] This is not an uncommon problem with translating Biblical Hebrew. For example, Exodus 12:15 literally says:

1. Seven days you shall eat unleavened bread,

1. Until this very day they do according to their former ways,
3. according to their statutes and their judgments,
2. they do not fear YHWH, and they do not do,
4. according to the Torah and commandments that YHWH commanded the children of Jacob. (2 Kings 17:34)[69]

The way the verse is structured in Hebrew lays emphasis on the Samaritans doing "according to **<u>their</u>** statutes and **<u>their</u>** judgments" but "they do not do" according to the Torah. When I finally understood this verse, it hit me that this was the solution to Matthew 23:3. Both verses had this seemingly inexplicable phrase "they do not do" which did not seem to fit. But it did fit when 2 Kings 17:34 was understood with correct Hebrew syntax. Yeshua was echoing the special style of 2 Kings 17:34 when he said about the Pharisees, "but according to <u>their</u> reforms (*takanot*) and <u>their</u> precedents (*ma'asim*) do not do, because they talk <u>but they do not do</u>" (Hebrew Matthew 23:3). 2 Kings 17:34 records a

2. but by the first day you shall completely remove leaven from your houses,
3. for anyone who eats leaven, that soul shall be cut off from Israel,
4. from the first day until the seventh day.

Obviously this verse must be translated into English with the clauses re-ordered as 1, 2, 4, 3. All the standard translations do this without leaving any trace of the eccentricity of the Hebrew syntax (sentence structure). An example of this same phenomenon in the New Testament is Revelation 20:4–5 in which the phrase "This is the first resurrection" belongs at the end of v.4, not the end of v.5; this is an example of Hebrew syntax preserved in the Greek text of Revelation. An almost comical example in the Torah is Genesis 14:12 which literally reads, "And they took Lot and his property, <u>the son of Abram's brother</u>," which obviously means, "And they took Lot <u>the son of Abram's brother</u> and his property."

69
1. עַד הַיּוֹם הַזֶּה הֵם עֹשִׂים כַּמִּשְׁפָּטִים הָרִאשֹׁנִים
3. כְּחֻקֹּתָם וּכְמִשְׁפָּטָם
2. אֵינָם יְרֵאִים אֶת יְהוָה וְאֵינָם עֹשִׂים
4. וְכַתּוֹרָה וְכַמִּצְוָה אֲשֶׁר צִוָּה יְהוָה אֶת בְּנֵי יַעֲקֹב אֲשֶׁר שָׂם שְׁמוֹ יִשְׂרָאֵל׃

very similar thing about the Samaritans who follow "their statutes and their judgments" but "do not do" Torah. **Yeshua was saying that like the Samaritans of old, the Pharisees have their own statutes and judgments which they follow, while at the same time they talk Torah but they do not do Torah.** To emphasize this, he borrowed the unique phrase from 2 Kings 17:34 talking about the sins of the Samaritans and applied this to the Pharisees.

Chapter 10
You Have Heard It Said

A few weeks after I realized the Samaritan connection, I was invited to present my findings before a small group in Jerusalem. As I shared my findings I became increasingly aware that in the Greek version Yeshua – what some might call, the "Greek Jesus" – had done away with many things in the Torah and promoted Phariseeism. On the other hand, the Hebrew Yeshua seemed to be trying to restore the Torah which had been covered over by years of Pharisaic-Rabbinic traditions and man-made laws. I found myself thinking out loud: Was the Hebrew Yeshua a Karaite?

When I was done sharing what I had learned, some of the audience members asked questions. One audience member asked how all this fit in with the series of teachings in which Yeshua says, "You have heard it said… but I say…". Weren't these teachings doing away with various things in the Torah? I had not thought about this so I said I would look into it and get back to him with an answer.

That night I read through the "You have heard it said…" passage in Matthew 5 in the Greek. It did seem to annul various commandments in the Torah. Maybe he was right? Maybe Yeshua did come to do away with parts of the Torah after all? As a Karaite I was not committed either way, but as a textual scholar the question nagged at my mind. If Yeshua came to do away with the Torah then how did this fit in with the "not one jot or tittle" passage in Matthew 5:17, which seems to uphold even the minutest points of Torah? I felt like I was missing something.

About a week later I sat down with a Messianic friend of mine and we read through Matthew 5 together. One section that was particularly problematic from my perspective was Matthew 5:33–37:

> (33) Again, you have heard that it was said to the people long ago, "Do not break your oath, but keep the oaths you have made to the Lord." (34) **<u>But I tell you, Do not swear at all</u>**: either by heaven, for it is God's throne; (35) or by the earth, for it is his footstool; or by Jerusalem, for it is the city of the Great King. (36) And do not swear by your head, for you cannot make even one hair white or black. (37) Simply let your "Yes" be "Yes," and your "No," "No"; anything beyond this comes from the evil one. (Matthew 5:33–37 [NIV])

The "Greek Jesus" was very clearly saying not to make vows but only to say "yes" or "no."

I explained to my Messianic friend that as a Karaite this was a sensitive topic for me. One of the things I had been taught by my rabbis was that it is utterly forbidden to say the name of the Creator. At first I accepted this doctrine, even after becoming a Karaite; it was so ingrained that it became second nature. But one day an old Karaite sage I used to study with named Mordecai Alfandari sat me down and asked me to read Exodus 3:15 out loud:

> And God said further to Moses, thus shall you say to the children of Israel, **YHWH**, the God of your fathers, the God of Abraham, the God of Isaac, and the God of Jacob has sent me to you, this is My name forever and this is My memorial from generation to generation. (Exodus 3:15)

As I read this verse out loud I realized how wrong I had been. Here it says explicitly that the eternal name of the Creator is Yehovah, pronounced by some as Yahweh, Yihweh, etc.[70] But following the Rabbanite ban on the name, I had read the verse as if it said, "Adonai (Lord)… this is My name forever and this is My memorial from generation to generation." The ban on the name had created a mental block which changed the eternal name to "Lord" even though the word YHWH יהוה was right there before me in the Hebrew text. When I realized this, the words of the prophet came to mind, "They have eyes but they do not see" (Jeremiah 5:21).

At the time, I remember wondering what this verse meant when it said that Yehovah is His "memorial" from generation to generation. I mean, it makes it sound like Yehovah is dead that He has a memorial! Later when I became fluent in Hebrew I discovered that this was simply a horrible translation. The Hebrew word usually translated "memorial" is *zikhri* זִכְרִי. This word comes from the root *zkr* ז.כ.ר. which actually has a broader meaning than simply "memorial." It means "to refer to something" either with the mind ("remember/ memorial") or with the mouth ("mention"). The same exact root appears in Exodus 23:13, which says, "…and the names of other gods you shall not **mention** (*tazkiru* תַזְכִּירוּ from the root *zkr* ז.כ.ר.) nor shall they be heard upon your mouth." So in Exodus 3:15 it really

[70] The reasons for my pronunciation of the name as Yehovah will be explained in my upcoming study on the divine name.

says, "this is my name for ever, this is *zikri*, my **mention**, from generation to generation." This means we are required by Scripture to *mention* Him by His eternal name Yehovah! This fits with the explicit commandment to swear by the name Yehovah. For example, Deuteronomy 6:13 "You shall fear YHWH your God, and you shall worship Him, **and in His name shall you swear**." This is a clear and explicit commandment to make oaths in the name of Yehovah. Similarly, Deuteronomy 10:20, "YHWH your God you shall fear, and Him shall you worship, and to him shall you cling, and in His name shall you swear."

The practice of swearing in the name of YHWH is something seen throughout the Tanach. For example, in 1 Kings 2:23 King Solomon vows by invoking the name of YHWH, "So shall YHWH do to me and even more…". He is basically laying a curse on himself that YHWH shall punish him in such and such a manner if he is lying or does not fulfill the terms of his vow. In 1 Samuel 20:3 we find David making a vow, "As YHWH lives…". There is actually a very important end-times prophecy in Jeremiah 12:16 related to the vow formula, "As YHWH lives":

> And it shall be if they nevertheless learn the way of My people to swear in My name "As YHWH lives," in the way that they taught My people to swear by Ba'al, then they shall be built into My people. (Jeremiah 12:16)

I was always fascinated by this prophecy because it is speaking to the Gentiles, not the Israelites! It's directed at those Gentiles who taught Israel to swear by Baal. If these Gentiles will learn to swear "As YHWH lives" then they will become a part of the covenant-nation. Obviously this has not happened yet. At this point most Israelites have forgotten how to swear "As YHWH lives" and I am not aware of too many Gentiles who do this either. But this is a promise that in the end-time the Gentiles will learn to swear in the name of YHWH and through this they will be built into Israel. This is why I was so surprised when I saw in the Greek Matthew (5:33–37) that Jesus did away with swearing, even saying that he who swears was of "the evil one." If this is really what Jesus said, then he would not only be annulling Torah but delaying the fulfillment of the end-times prophecy in Jeremiah. Before I passed final judgment on Yeshua I decided to double check in the Hebrew. What I found there was a small difference but it was the difference between day and night. In the Hebrew Matthew, Yeshua says,

> (33) You have further heard what was said by the ancients, "you shall not swear falsely by my name" [Leviticus 19:12] but you must pay your vow to YHWH [paraphrase of Deuteronomy 23:21]. (34) But I say to you, that you must not swear by anything <u>falsely</u>, not by heaven which is the throne of God, (35) nor by the earth which is His footstool, nor by [Jerusalem] which is His city, (36) nor by your head because you cannot make one hair white or black, (37) But let your yes be yes and your no, no. Anything added to this is evil. (Hebrew Matthew 5:33–37)[71]

What Yeshua is saying in the Hebrew is not to swear <u>falsely</u>! The Torah had said in Leviticus 19:12 not to swear falsely in the name of YHWH. It seems that some Pharisees took this as permission to swear falsely as long as the name of YHWH was not used. This strange doctrine was based on an over-

[71] Matthew 5:33–37 in Shem-Tov's Hebrew Matthew:

(33) עוֹד שְׁמַעְתֶּם מָה שֶׁנֶּאֱמַר לַקַּדְמוֹנִים "לֹא תִשָּׁבְעוּ בִשְׁמִי לַשָּׁקֶר" וְתָשִׁיב לַ[יְ]ה[וָ]ה] שְׁבוּעָתֶךָ: (34) וַאֲנִי אוֹמֵר לָכֶם לְבִלְתִּי הִשָּׁבַע בְּשׁוּם עִנְיַין לַשָּׁוְא, לֹא בַּשָּׁמַיִם שֶׁכִּסֵּא אֱלֹ[הִ]ים הִיא: (35) וְלֹא בָּאָרֶץ שֶׁהֲדוֹם רַגְלָיו הוּא, לֹא בַּשָּׁמַיִם [צ״ל בִּירוּשָׁלַםִ] שֶׁעִיר אֱלֹ[הִ]ים הִיא: (36) וְלֹא בְּרֹאשְׁךָ שֶׁלֹּא תוּכַל לַעֲשׂוֹת שֵׂעָר אֶ[חָ]ד] לָבָן אוֹ שָׁחוֹר: (37) אֲבָל יִהְיוּ דִּבְרֵיכֶם הֵן הֵן וְגַם לֹא לֹא. כֹּל הַנּוֹסָף עַל זֶה הוּא רָע:

The Rabbinical "euphemisms" אלקים and ה׳ have been restored to the original אלהים and יהוה (respectively) in all of the present quotations from Shem-Tov's Hebrew Matthew. See also the discussion on swearing in Howard 1995 pp. 213–214. Compare also James 5:12.

literalization of Leviticus 19:12, "you shall not swear falsely by My name." The Pharisees took this to mean that as long as you do not swear by the name YHWH, you are free to swear falsely. Yeshua protests that it is forbidden to swear falsely by anything. It does not matter if the vow is "by YHWH" or "by Jerusalem." Any vow "by anything" is binding. If you say, yes, I swear to do such and such, no matter what you vowed by, you must keep your word. The same holds true if you vow, No, I swear not to do such and such; you must stand by it.

Yeshua ends his exhortation with a paraphrase of Deuteronomy 4:2 which says not to add to the Torah: "Anything added to this is evil." Yeshua is reaffirming this basic Torah principle, probably to silence anyone who might think he is adding to the Torah. The fact that he includes swearing falsely by anything in the prohibition "You shall not swear falsely by My name" (Leviticus 19:12) is not intended as an addition to the Torah. Instead he is simply bringing out the underlying principle of the Torah commandment which is to prohibit false vows of any kind, not just those made in the name of YHWH. Yeshua reiterates the prohibition not to add to the Torah to make it clear to his disciples that he is *not* adding to the Torah nor would he ever do that because *anything* added to the Torah is evil! The difference between the Greek and the Hebrew is fundamental! The Greek IESOUS is doing away with whole commandments from the Torah while the Hebrew Yeshua seems to be reaffirming Torah. [72]

A few weeks later I met with some Messianic friends who had been at the first meeting where I shared on the Hebrew Matthew. They had asked if we could get together and look in more detail at some of the issues in the text of Hebrew Matthew.

[72] IESOUS ᾽Ιησοῦς is the Greek form of Jesus, which differs from the Hebrew Yeshua יֵשׁוּעַ.

As a Karaite I always insist that people show me where something is written so I can see for myself and I was happy to oblige others with the same request. We looked at the question of the swearing and I shared what I had found. One of them asked if I knew of any Pharisaic opinion that said a vow was only binding if the name of YHWH was used. I had checked this question, but could not find any reference to this in the Talmud. Now anyone who has studied the Talmud knows that on every conceivable point of religious law there are usually two diametrically opposed opinions. One rabbi may say that a certain thing is clean while another will rule it to be unclean. In Pharisaic thinking this is not inconsistent with the claim that the Oral Torah was revealed on Mt. Sinai. The Talmud itself explains, that when two rabbis present diametrically opposing views, "both these and those are the words of the living God."[73] In other words, when God revealed the "Oral" Torah on Mt. Sinai he gave Moses two contradictory rulings on every detail of law. Some rabbis explain that the first opinion is for the present era while the second opinion will become operative only after the future Messiah comes. Despite this diversity of opinions in the Talmud, I did not find any evidence that the Pharisees believed that a vow which omits the name of YHWH is non-binding. I suggested that perhaps the Pharisaic opinion that considered a vow without the name to be non-binding was simply not recorded in the Talmud. We know many Pharisaic teachings were lost. Indeed, at least one-third of the Jerusalem Talmud has been completely lost![74] As these words came out of my mouth, I had Hebrew Matthew 23 in

[73] "Rabbi Abba said in the name of Samuel: For three years the House of Shammai and the House of Hillel were divided. Each one said the law is according to us. Then a voice came out from heaven and said: 'Both these and those are the words of the living God.'" (*Babylonian Talmud*, Erubin 13b)

[74] Specifically, the Jerusalem Talmud *orders* of Kodashim and Tohorot (except for three chapters), mentioned by medieval authors, are no longer extant.

front of me and I looked down and there was confirmation of what I had suggested as a theory! I began to read:

> (16) Woe to you, you blind **chairs**, who say that he who swears by the sanctuary is not obligated but he who vows by anything that is sanctified to the sanctuary building is obligated to pay. (17) Mad men and blind men! Which is greater, the sanctuary or the thing which is sanctified to the sanctuary? (18) And [you say] he who vows by the altar is not obligated but he who vows to bring a sacrifice must give it. (19) Which is greater, the sacrifice or the altar? The sanctuary or the sacrifice? (20) He who swears by the altar swears by it and by all that is in it. (Hebrew Matthew 23:16–20)[75]

Throughout this passage Yeshua is speaking to the Pharisees. Earlier he had said that they sit in the seat of Moses and now he calls them **in the Hebrew** "you blind chairs"; they sit in the seat or "chair" of Moses but they are proverbially blind. Then he criticizes them for saying that if a person swears "by the sanctuary" or "by the altar" he is not bound by this oath. This is exactly the view that Yeshua is speaking against in Matthew 5:33–37 when he says not to swear falsely by anything not even "by Jerusalem." What is significant about Matthew 23:16–20 is that the Hebrew and Greek are not substantially different. In both texts Yeshua says that oaths and vows are binding no matter what they are made by. He gives no hint that he is against making vows nor does he indicate that a person who swears "by the sanctuary" or vows "by the altar" is of "the evil one." On the contrary, in

[75] Matthew 23:16–20 in Shem-Tov's Hebrew Matthew:
(16) אוי לָכֶם מוֹשְׁבֵי הַעִוְרִים אֲשֶׁר תֹּאמְרוּ שֶׁהַנִּשְׁבָּע בַּהֵיכָל אֵינוֹ חַיָּיב וַאֲשֶׁר יִדּוֹר בְּאֵיזֶה דָּבָר שֶׁהוּא נִקְדָּשׁ לַבִּנְיָין הַהֵיכָל חַיָּיב לְשַׁלֵּם: (17) מְשׁוּגָּעִים וְעִוְרִים! אֵיזֶה יוֹתֵר גָּדוֹל? הַהֵיכָל אוֹ דָּבָר הַנִּקְדָּשׁ לַהֵיכָל? (18) וְ[תֹאמְרוּ] אֲשֶׁר יִשָּׁבַע בַּמִּזְבֵּחַ אֵינוֹ חַיָּיב וְהַנִּשְׁבָּע שֶׁיַּקְרִיב קָרְבָּן חַיָּיב לָתֵת: (19) אֵיזֶה יוֹתֵר? הַקָּרְבָּן אוֹ הַמִּזְבֵּחַ? הַמִּקְדָּשׁ אוֹ הַקָּרְבָּן? (20) אֲשֶׁר יִשָּׁבַע בַּמִּזְבֵּחַ נִשְׁבָּע בּוֹ וּבְכֹל מַה שֶּׁבְּתוֹכוֹ:

both the Hebrew and the Greek, Yeshua upholds the principle behind the prohibition not to swear falsely in the name of YHWH, which is really a prohibition against any false oath. Here again the Hebrew Yeshua was trying to return the people to the Torah after the Pharisees led them astray.

Chapter 11
A New Understanding

Through all these investigations I have been repeatedly surprised about what I have learned about Yeshua. I still do not believe Yeshua to be the Messiah; like all Karaites I eagerly await the coming of the anointed Davidic king who will reign as king over Israel, ushering in an era of eternal peace (Isaiah 11; Ezekiel 34:24–25; even Luke 1:32–33). To my knowledge Yeshua has yet to fulfill this fundamental criterion of the Davidic Messiah. However, my understanding of who Yeshua was as an historical person has changed. I once thought him to be a usurper who came to do away with Torah.[76] Yet the more I study the Hebrew

[76] The portrayal of Yeshua as a usurper is the opinion of the Talmud:

> On the eve of the Passover Yeshu was hanged. For forty days before the execution took place, a herald went forth and cried, 'He is going forth to be stoned because he has practised sorcery and enticed Israel to apostacy. Any one who can say anything in his favour, let him come forward and plead on his behalf.' But since nothing was brought forward in his favour he was hanged on the eve of the Passover! (*Babylonian Talmud*, Sanhedrin 43a (uncensored version) [Soncino Translation])

Matthew, the more I find that whenever Jesus seems to be doing away with Torah in the Greek, Yeshua ends up upholding Torah in the Hebrew. It seems more and more that Yeshua may have been a 1st Century Karaite opposing the man-made laws of the Rabbis and returning people to Torah. Perhaps only more research will decisively prove if he really was.

I will close with the words of the 10th Century Karaite sage Jacob Kirkisani:

> Some of the Karaites say that Yeshua was a good man and that his way was that of Zadok, Anan, and others; and that the Rabbanites conspired against him and killed him just as they sought to kill Anan also, but without success.[77]

Kirkisani is saying that the Rabbis conspired to kill Yeshua because he tried to return people to Torah just as "Zadok" and Anan did. "Zadok" is a reference to the Sadducees, the high priests during Second Temple times who traced their lineage to Zadok, the high priest under David (2 Samuel 8:17). Zadok was an important high priest because he was the first to serve in Solomon's Temple and it was he who "anointed" Solomon as king (1 Kings 1:39). So Zadok became the symbol of a high priest who had the legitimacy to serve in the Temple and to anoint the Messianic king. Ezekiel 44:15 mentions "the Levitical priests, **Sons of Zadok**, who kept the instruction of My sanctuary when the children of Israel strayed from me." The name "Sadducees" is simply the Greek form of the Hebrew *tsadokim* צָדוֹקִים which means "Sons of Zadok" (Ezekiel 44:15). Today the

This is also the opinion of some Karaites, such as the 9th Century sage Benjamin Nahawendi who believed Yeshua to be one of the false prophets mentioned in Daniel 11:14. Other Karaites disagreed, see below.

[77] Translation adapted from Kirkisani p. 135. Interestingly, Kirkisani writes out Yeshua's name in Hebrew as *Yeshu'a* ישוע.

Sadducees/Sons of Zadok are best-known for their denial of the resurrection of the dead. But this was only the view of one faction of Sadducees who became predominant in the 1st Century CE. Earlier Sadducees, such as the author of *2 Maccabees*, embraced the doctrine of resurrection of the dead on the basis of such explicit verses as Daniel 12:2 and Psalms 133:3.[78] The one thing we know all Sadducees unequivocally agreed upon was their commitment to Torah and rejection of Pharisaic innovations. Josephus, the 1st Century CE Jewish historian writes,

> What I would now explain is this, that the Pharisees have delivered to the people a great many observances by succession from their fathers, which are not written in the laws of Moses; and for that reason it is that the Sadducees reject them, and say that we are to esteem those observances to be obligatory which are in the written word, but are not to observe what are derived from the tradition of our forefathers. (Josephus Flavius, *Antiquities of the Jews* 13.10.6 (13.297) [Whiston Translation p. 281]).[79]

So, the fundamental difference between the Pharisees and the Sadducees was that the Pharisees promoted man-made traditions while the Sadducees rejected these innovations and clung to the

[78] The theme of resurrection appears repeatedly throughout 2 Maccabees, for example, 7:9, 11, 14, 23, 29, 36; 12:40–45; 14:46. It is indeed a mystery how the later Sadducees failed to understand such clear verses as Daniel 12:2 which unequivocally teach of a future resurrection.

[79] Marcus Translation p. 377: "For the present I wish merely to explain that the Pharisees had passed on to the people certain regulations handed down by former generations and not recorded in the Laws of Moses, for which reason they are rejected by the Sadducaean group, who hold that only those regulations should be considered valid which were written down (in Scripture), and that those which had been handed down by former generations (Lit. "by the fathers.") need not be observed."

written Scripture alone.[80] Kirkisani is saying that like the early Sadducees (who still believed in resurrection of the dead) Yeshua opposed the man-made laws of the Rabbis and tried to return people to the Torah.

Kirkisani also compares Yeshua to Anan.[81] As already mentioned, Anan was criticized by most Karaites because even though he rejected Rabbinical authority he clung to the irrational methods of interpretation used by the Rabbis. However, Kirkisani was particularly sympathetic to Anan and gave him an A+ for effort for trying to return people to Torah. It seems Kirkisani also gave Yeshua an A+ for effort for trying to return people to Torah. I wonder what Kirkisani would have said if he had read Shem-Tov's Hebrew Matthew?

[80] In Matthew 16:6 Yeshua warns of "the leaven of the Pharisees and of the Sadducees." It is significant that in the two parallel passages in Mark 8:15 and Luke 12:1 no mention is made of the Sadducees, only of the Pharisees.

[81] A major point of comparison between Yeshua and Anan is that, according to legend, the Rabbis also tried to have Anan killed for returning people to Torah, see Appendix 3.

Appendix 1
The Testimony of Papias

When my colleague at the university first told me that, according to some scholars, the Gospel of Matthew was originally written in Hebrew, I thought he was pulling my leg. This was before I knew about Shem-Tov's Hebrew Matthew so at the time I thought that this sounded pretty incredible. One thing that everyone knows about the New Testament is that it is documented by numerous papyri fragments and over 5000 manuscripts dating back to the first few centuries after it was written.[82] I knew that all these ancient papyri and manuscripts of the New Testament were in Greek. So how could Matthew have been written in Hebrew?! Another thing I had been taught was that the book of Matthew is quoted in Greek by numerous "Church Fathers." The term "Church Father" refers to early Christian writers in the first six centuries CE. Now if Matthew had really been written in Hebrew, then surely someone back in those early days must have remembered this! And if the Greek text was such a bad

[82] Epp p. 5

translation from the Hebrew, then the Church Fathers must have said something about this. As these words came out of my mouth my colleague looked at me across his desk with a curled brow and said, "But the Church Fathers **did** say that Matthew wrote his gospel in Hebrew! Didn't you know that?!" Well I didn't, so I asked him what he was talking about. He told me to meet him the next day at the Mt. Scopus library where we went to a room with a large microfiche-set containing all the writings of the Church Fathers in the original Greek. My colleague spent a few minutes flipping through the microfiches and eventually found what he was looking for. He showed me the words of a little known Church Father named Papias quoted by Eusebius. Papias had been the bishop of Hierapolis, a town in Asia Minor and lived about 60–130 CE. Much of what Papias knew about Yeshua and his disciples came directly from the testimony of people who had studied under the original disciples. Among the people Papias spoke to directly was "John the presbyter," the author of the *Gospel of John*.[83] Based on his inside information, Papias reports matter-of-factly:

> Matthew collected the oracles [literally: "words"] **in the Hebrew language**, and each interpreted them as best he could.[84]

[83] Quoted in Eusebius, *Ecclesiastical History*, 3:39 (Lake Translation pp. 290–299). Papias is also called "the hearer of John." Eusebius is uncertain if this is the same John that is said to have written Revelation.

[84] Lake Translation p. 297. Cruse Translation p. 127: "Matthew composed his history in the Hebrew dialect, and everyone translated it as he was able." Deferrari Translation vol. 1 p. 206: "Now Matthew collected the oracles in the Hebrew language, and each one interpreted them as he was able." Ματθαῖος μὲν οὖν Ἑβραΐδι διαλέκτῳ τὰ λόγια συνετάξατο, ἡρμήνευσεν δ᾽ αὐτὰ ὡς ἦν δυνατὸς ἕκαστος (Lake ed. p. 296). See also Howard 1995 pp. 155–160. On the description of the "Gospel" of Matthew as "oracles/ history" *logia* λόγια see Grintz pp. 41–42. This word literally means "words."

My colleague explained that the Greek word *hermeneusen* ἡρμήνευσεν "interpreted" can also mean "translated," just as in English an "interpreter" is someone who translates.[85] So there it was in black and white. Papias was saying Matthew wrote his gospel in Hebrew and speakers of different languages did their best to interpret or translate it into their own languages. Apparently Papias realized that some of the ancient translations of Matthew's Hebrew Gospel were none too accurate and this is why he says that "each translated them as best he could." So not only was it known in ancient times that Matthew was originally written in Hebrew, but it was also widely recognized that the Greeks and other non-Hebrews had a difficult time translating Hebrew Matthew into Greek and other languages.

[85] See Liddell and Scott p. 690 under the verb *hermeneuo* ἑρμηνεύω "*interpret* foreign tongues" and the related noun *hermeneia* ἑρμηνεία "translation." Cruse Translation p. 127 also renders this word as "translate."

Appendix 2
The Abomination of Desolation

When I sent out the draft of this book for comments and suggestions, one of the strangest replies I got was that Shem-Tov's Hebrew Matthew is actually anti-Christian (or: anti-Yeshua). How could a book of the New Testament be anti-Christian? The person who told me this explained that Shem-Tov's Hebrew Matthew refers to the Gospel of Matthew as the "Antichrist" and as the "abomination of desolation." This bizarre accusation derives from a rumor being spread across the internet based on a misunderstanding of Hebrew Matthew 24:14–15.[86] In the Greek, this passage reads:

> (14) And this gospel of the kingdom shall be preached in all the world for a witness unto all nations; and then shall the end come. (15) When ye therefore shall see the **abomination of desolation**, spoken of by Daniel the prophet, stand in the holy place, (whoso readeth, let him understand:) (Matthew 24:14–15 [KJV])

[86] This rumor was undoubtedly inspired by the discussion in Howard 1995 p. 215.

These verses speak about the "abomination of desolation" which is also mentioned in the end-of-days prophecies in Daniel 11:31 and 12:11. In his translation of Shem-Tov's Hebrew Matthew, George Howard translates these same verses as follows:

> (14) And this gospel, that is, evungili, will be preached in all the earth for a witness concerning me to all the nations and then **the end** will come. (15) **This is the Anti-Christ and this is the abomination which desolates** which was spoken of by Daniel [as] standing in the holy place. Let the one who reads understand. (Hebrew Matthew 24:14–15 [Howard's Translation])

According to the internet rumor, Shem-Tov's Hebrew Matthew is identifying the Gospel of Matthew itself as the "Antichrist" and the "abomination which desolates." Were this really the case, why would v.14 say to preach this gospel in all the earth? If read in context, Shem-Tov's Hebrew Matthew is really saying **"the end" will be marked by the "abomination of desolation"** spoken of by the prophet Daniel.

The "Antichrist" in Hebrew Matthew 24:15 can be better understood if we first consider one of the limitations of Howard's translation. Shem-Tov's Hebrew Matthew contains many Greek and Latin "glosses" which were added by Shem-Tov himself. A gloss is usually one or two words added into the margin of an ancient text. These non-Hebrew glosses served to familiarize Jews with Greek and Latin terms. The goal was to equip Jews forced to debate in the public Disputations against the Catholics, who would be using Greek and Latin terminology. For some reason, Howard chose not to identify these non-Hebrew glosses as such in his translation. If you can read the Hebrew text it does not really matter. A Hebrew reader can immediately identify these glosses, because it is obvious they are Greek or Latin words written in Hebrew letters. But anyone relying entirely on the English translation has no way of distinguishing between the original Hebrew text and the non-Hebrew glosses added by Shem-Tov. In the verses in question, the word "Antichrist" actually appears in the Hebrew as a Greek word written with Hebrew letters, which makes it clear that this is one of Shem-Tov's glosses. So what it actually says in Hebrew is as follows:

> (14) You must preach this good news [Gloss: "in the foreign tongue, Evangelium"] in all the earth as a testimony concerning me to all the nations, and then shall come **the end**. (15) **[Gloss: "This is, the Antichrist"] and this is the abomination of desolation** spoken of by Daniel, which stands in the holy place, and he who reads shall understand. (Hebrew Matthew 24:14–15 [My Translation])

The word "Antichrist" is actually a Greek gloss that explains the Greek equivalent of the Hebrew phrase "abomination of desolation" to the Jewish debaters. In other words, when the Jews stand in the public Disputation and hear the Catholics talking about the "Antichrist" they now know that this is what Jews call in Hebrew the "abomination of desolation." Originally glosses were written in the margin and later they were inserted into the body of the text.[87] In this case, the non-Hebrew "Antichrist" was erroneously placed before "abomination of desolation" instead of after it, a very common error. But it is still clear that the word "Antichrist" is one of Shem-Tov's glosses, because it is obvious in Hebrew that it is a foreign word, even though it appears in Hebrew letters as *antichristos* אנטיקריסטוש.[88] In any event, with or without Shem-Tov's "Antichrist," the "abomination of

[87] In some manuscripts of Shem-Tov's Hebrew Matthew glosses can still be seen written in the margins.

[88] Compare Franz Delitzsch's Hebrew translation of the Greek New Testament in which the term Antichrist is translated into proper Hebrew as שֹׂטֵן הַמָּשִׁיחַ *soten hamashiach.*

desolation" in Hebrew Matthew 23:15 identifies "the end" spoken of in v.14. What it is saying is that Daniel's "abomination of desolation" will signal "the end."

Appendix 3
Absolute Authority of the Rabbis

The incident of Rabbi Eliezer in the *Babylonian Talmud*, Baba Metsia 59b (see p. 14 above) holds a central place in modern Rabbinic theology. Maimonides (Rambam), a 12th Century Rabbinic theologian, explains based on this incident, that any prophet who prophesies that the Rabbis are wrong on even a minor point of interpretation, must be executed:

> If there are 1000 prophets, all of them of the stature of Elijah and Elisha, giving a certain interpretation, and 1001 rabbis giving the opposite interpretation, you shall "incline after the majority" (Exodus 23:2) and the law is according to the 1001 rabbis, not according to the 1000 venerable prophets. And thus our Sages said, "By God, if we heard the matter directly from the mouth of Joshua the son of Nun, we would not obey him nor would we listen to him!" The Sages said further, "If Elijah comes and tells us, 'The levirate obligation is cancelled through a shoe' (see Deuteronomy 25:9), we will listen to him [because this is what the Oral Law

> teaches], but if he says it is cancelled through a sandal, we will not listen to him [because this is contrary to the Oral Law]." …And so if a prophet testifies that the Holy-One, Blessed be He, told him that the law of a certain commandment is such and such, or [even] that the reasoning of a certain sage is correct, that prophet must be executed… as it is written, "it is not in heaven" (Deuteronomy 30:12). Thus God did not permit us to learn from the prophets, only from the Rabbis who are men of logic and reason. (Maimonides, pp. 27–28)[89]

Maimonides emphasizes that a prophet who prophesies something contrary to the Oral Law, **even if Scripture agrees with the prophet**, that prophet must be executed:

> He who prophecies in the name… if he changes anything in the Oral Law, even if the plain meaning of Scripture supports what he says, for example, if he says that when the Torah says "you shall cut off her hand; [show no pity]" (Deuteronomy 25:12) that it literally means cutting off the hand and not a monetary fine as we are taught by the Oral Law, and that prophet attributes his statement to prophecy saying, "The Holy-One, Blesses be He, told me that the commandment that says, 'you shall cut off her hand' is to be understood at face value," that prophet shall be executed through strangulation…" (Maimonides, pp. 16–17)[90]

[89] Compare Rosner Translation pp. 33–34.

[90] Compare Rosner Translation pp. 15–17.

This means that when the future messiah comes and tells the Rabbis it is permissible to eat meat and milk together, but forbidden to boil a sheep or goat in its mother's milk, the Rabbis will try to have him killed!

Appendix 4
The Text of Matthew 23:2-3

King James Version

(2) The scribes and the Pharisees sit in Moses' seat: (3) All therefore whatsoever **they** bid you observe, that observe and do; but do not ye after their works: for they say, and do not.

Greek Matthew

(2) λέγων, Ἐπὶ τῆς Μωϋσέως καθέδρας ἐκάθισαν οἱ γραμματεῖς καὶ οἱ Φαρισαῖοι. (3) πάντα οὖν ὅσα ἐὰν εἴπωσιν ὑμῖν ποιήσατε καὶ τηρεῖτε, κατὰ δὲ τὰ ἔργα αὐτῶν μὴ ποιεῖτε· λέγουσιν γὰρ καὶ οὐ ποιοῦσιν.

Shem-Tov's Hebrew Matthew

(2) לֵאמֹר עַל כִּסֵּא מֹשֶׁה יֵשְׁבוּ הַפִּירוּשִׁים וְהַחֲכָמִים: (3) וְעַתָּה כֹּל אֲשֶׁר יֹאמַר לָכֶם שִׁמְרוּ וַעֲשׂוּ וּבְתַקָּנוֹתֵיהֶם וּמַעֲשֵׂיהֶם אַל תַּעֲשׂוּ שֶׁהֵם אוֹמְרִים וְהֵם אֵינָם עוֹשִׂים:[91]

Shem-Tov's Hebrew Matthew (Transliteration)

(2) Le-mor, Al ki-se Mo-she yesh-vu ha-pi-ru-shim ve-ha-cha-cha-mim. (3) Ve-a-ta, kol a-sher yo-mar la-chem shim-ru va-asu u-ve-ta-ka-no-te-hem u-ma-a-se-hem al ta-a-su she-hem om-rim ve-hem e-nam o-sim.

Shem-Tov's Hebrew Matthew (Translation)

Saying, the Pharisees and sages sit upon the seat of Moses. Therefore all that **he** says to you diligently do, but according to their reforms (*takanot*) and their precedents (*ma'asim*) do not do, because they talk but they do not do.

Based on Shem-Tov's Hebrew, the Greek of verse 3 should have read something like:

πάντα οὖν ὅσα ἐὰν **εἴπῃ** ὑμῖν ποιήσατε καὶ τηρεῖτε, κατὰ δὲ τὰ ἔργα αὐτῶν **καὶ τὰς παραδόσεις αὐτῶν** μὴ ποιεῖτε· λέγουσιν γὰρ καὶ οὐ ποιοῦσιν.

The main difference is that the surviving Greek text contains the 3rd plural aorist active subjunctive form *eiposin* εἴπωσιν "they said," whereas it should have had 3rd singular aorist active

[91] Adapted from Howard 1987 p. 112. I have checked the Hebrew text with the British Library manuscript (Add. 26964). The Shem-Tov text is without vowels. Vowels were added by myself.

subjunctive *eipei* εἴπῃ "he said," which would have been equivalent to the reading in Shem-Tov's Hebrew Matthew.

Even those who deny the antiquity of Shem-Tov's Hebrew Matthew must admit the superiority of this reading. Horbury, who dates Shem-Tov's Hebrew Matthew to the Middle Ages in what appears to be the only *serious* attempt at challenging Howard's evidence, admits that: "very old Christian readings could survive in Hebrew Gospel quotations in Jewish anti-Christian polemic" (Horbury p. 736). In other words, whatever the origin of Shem-Tov's Hebrew Matthew, it clearly contains early readings not found in the surviving Greek text.

The surviving Greek text is also missing the words *kai tas paradoseis auton* καὶ τὰς παραδόσεις αὐτῶν "and according to their traditions." I have reconstructed this missing Greek phrase based on Matthew 15:2–3, 6, in which the word *paradosis* παράδοσις "tradition" is paralleled in Shem-Tov's Hebrew by *takanot*. Josephus uses the same exact Greek word when he describes the Pharisaic Oral Law (Josephus Flavius, *Antiquities of the Jews* 13.10.6 (13.297)). It is possible that *paradosis* παράδοσις was the accepted Greek term for the Oral Law!

Appendix 5
A Glossary of Shem-Tov's Hebrew Matthew 23:2-3

"saying" אמר Qal infinitive construct	לֵאמֹר
"on, upon"	עַל
"seat, throne"	כִּסֵּא
"Moses"	מֹשֶׁה
"they sit" ישב Qal future (imperfect) 3rd masculine plural or "they sat" ישב Qal past (perfect) 3rd masculine plural compare Jeremiah 6:23; see also Grintz p. 39.	יֵשְׁבוּ or possibly יָשְׁבוּ
"the Pharisees" (sg פִּירוּשִׁי) variant form of הַפְּרוּשִׁים	הַפִּירוּשִׁים
"and the sages"	וְהַחֲכָמִים
"and now, therefore"	וְעַתָּה
"all"	כֹּל
"that"	אֲשֶׁר
"he says" אמר Qal future (imperfect) 3rd masculine	יֹאמַר

singular Note: "future tense" (imperfect) can mean future or present.	
"to you"	לָכֶם
literally: "keep!" שמר Qal imperative 2nd masculine plural When combined with "וַעֲשׂוּ" it can have an adverbial value "diligently," compare Deuteronomy 5:32	שִׁמְרוּ
"and do!" עשׂה Qal imperative 2nd masculine plural	וַעֲשׂוּ
"and according to their *takanot*" יהם = possessive plural suffix "their"	וּבְתַקָּנוֹתֵיהֶם
"and their *ma'asim*" יהם = possessive plural suffix "their"	וּמַעֲשֵׂיהֶם
"do not"	אַל
"you shall do" עשׂה Qal future (imperfect) 2nd masculine plural	תַּעֲשׂוּ
"because they"	שֶׁהֵם
"they say" אמר Qal participle masculine plural	אוֹמְרִים
"but they" (ו + הם) ו often has meaning of "but"; this is called ו"ו הניגוד *vav* of contrast.	וְהֵם
"they (do) not" (אין + ם) ם = pronominal suffix "they"	אֵינָם
"they do" עשׂה Qal participle masculine plural	עוֹשִׂים

Glossary of Terms

Adonai – "Lord". Hebrew epithet of Yehovah. Later used as a replacement for the name Yehovah. Whenever a Pharisee sees the word Yehovah in Scripture, he reads it as if it was written Adonai. See *Ban on Divine Name.*

Akiva, Rabbi – Leading Pharisee Rabbi of the Early 2nd Century CE. Akiva was famous for deriving meaning from a single Hebrew letter. In 132 CE he declared the Jewish rebel leader Simeon Bar-Cochba to be the Messiah. Rabbi Akiva was eventually executed by the Romans after the defeat of Bar-Cochba.

Anan – 8th Century CE Jewish leader who attained religious freedom for non-Talmudic Jews under Islamic rule. Although he did reject the absolute authority of the Rabbis, Anan was not a Karaite because he accepted the irrational methods of interpretation taught by the Pharisees. Anan's followers were called *Ananites.*

Ananites – Followers of the teachings of 8th Century Jewish teacher Anan. The Ananites continued down at least until the 10th Century CE.

Aramaic – Language of the Arameans ("Syrians"). Aramaic is a Semitic language similar to Hebrew. The relationship between Hebrew and Aramaic is roughly the relationship between German and English (both Germanic languages). Parts of Daniel (2:4–7:28) and Ezra (4:8–6:18; 7:12–26) are written in Aramaic along with Genesis 31:47 (two words) and Jeremiah 10:11. After the return from Babylon, Aramaic gradually replaced Hebrew as the language of many Jews.

Aramaisms – Aramaic thought patterns translated literally into another language such as Greek.

Ashkenazim – Jews from European Christian countries. Ashkenazim have their own traditions that differ from the Sephardim. Also called: European Jews or Occidental Jews.

Ba'al Shem-Tov – (1698–1760) – Ukrainian-born founder of *Hasidism.* A supposed miracle-worker, he was the first *Hasidic Rebbe.*

Babylonian Talmud – Central pillar of the Oral Law. The Babylonian Talmud was compiled in Babylonia and completed around 500 CE by Ravina and Rav Ashi. It contains Pharisaic discussions about every conceivable point of law, both biblical and Pharisaic. The starting point of these discussions is often an attempt to explain the meaning of the Mishnah.

Ban on Divine Name – Pharisaic law instituted sometime in the 2nd Century CE. According to the ban, it is forbidden to say the name "Yehovah" even in prayer or when reading from the Torah. As a rule, Pharisees replace the name "Yehovah" with the epithet *Adonai* (Lord).

Benjamin Nahawendi – 9th Century Karaite sage who lived in Nahawend in Persia.

Biblical Hebrew – Language of the Tanach (Old Testament). Biblical Hebrew was spoken in ancient Israel. After the return from Babylonia, Biblical Hebrew was gradually replaced with Aramaic and what became known later as Mishnaic Hebrew.

Chorazin – Also: Korazin. Town on the shore of the Sea of Galilee in northern Israel. Yeshua taught in the synagogue of Chorazin (Matthew 11:21; Luke 10:13) and archaeologists have uncovered a "Seat of Moses" from that synagogue.

Commandments of Our Rabbis – Another name for *Takanot.*

Commandments of the Torah – Pharisaic term to describe laws derived from the Torah (albeit usually through their irrational methods of interpretation). Opposite of "Commandments of Our Rabbis."

Custom – Any tradition practiced by an entire Jewish community for an extended period of time which then becomes binding law. Technically, any practice performed on three consecutive occasions which then becomes binding. An example of a binding custom is the wearing of the *Kippah* (skullcap).

Daniel al-Kumisi – 9th Century CE Karaite sage. Kumisi was born in Kumis in Persia and immigrated to Jerusalem around 880.

Dead Sea Scrolls – Ancient scrolls dating from the end of Second Temple Era mostly written by Essene Jews and found near the Dead Sea beginning in 1947. The Dead Sea Scrolls provide historians with a unique glimpse into 1st Century CE Judaism in the Land of Israel. Prior to the discovery of the scrolls, the primary information about 1st Century Judaism was derived from sources such as the Mishnah and the Talmud which were written down long afterwards.

Disputations – Debates in the Middle Ages in which the Jews were forced to defend their faith against Catholic attacks. The Disputations were often a pretext for Catholic persecution.

Divine Name – Yehovah. See *Ban on Divine Name.*

Eliezer, Rabbi – Rabbi Eliezer ben Hyrcanus. Greatest Rabbinical sage of the late 1st Century CE and teacher of Rabbi Akiva. According to the Talmud, Rabbi Eliezer summoned miracles to prove to the other rabbis that his legal rulings were correct. The Rabbis rejected his miracles and excommunicated him.

European Jews – Another name for *Ashkenazim.*

Eusebius – (c. 260–341) – Eusebius Pamphili, Bishop of Casarea on the northern coast of Israel.

Even Bochan – Literally: "Test Stone". Name of Shem-Tov Ibn Shaprut's polemical work written in 1380. Hebrew Matthew was added to Even Bochan as an appendix.

Feast of Booths – Another name for Feast of Tabernacles. Also called Chag Ha-Sukkot. Seven-day Biblical pilgrimage-feast beginning on the 15th day of the 7th Month.

Gamaliel, Rabban – Rabban Gamaliel II. Leading Pharisee in the late 1st Century CE. The grandson of Gamaliel I mentioned in Acts 5:34; 22:3.

Gemara – Aramaic name for the *Talmud.*

Gloss – An explanatory note, often added in the margin of a manuscript, often explaining the meaning of a word in another language. The glosses in Shem-Tov's Hebrew Matthew give the Greek or Latin equivalents of many Hebrew terms.

Hakhel ceremony – Literally: "Gathering". A ceremony commanded in the Torah (Deuteronomy 31:7–13) to be held every seventh year over the Feast of Booths. At the Hakhel ceremony the Torah is read to the entire Israelite nation including men, women, children, and the strangers. The purpose of the Hakhel Ceremony was to teach the average Israelite the laws of the Torah.

Hasidic Rebbe – Leader of any number of *Hasidic* sects. Beginning in the 18th Century, many towns in Eastern Europe had a local "Rebbe" who gathered a following of *Hasidim* around him. The Rebbe's claim to authority was usually the miracles he performed or descent from an earlier miracle worker. The recently deceased Rabbi Schneerson of Lubavitch, whose followers claim him to be the

Messiah, is an example of a *Hasidic* Rebbe. Another example, is Rabbi Nachman of Braslav.

Hasidim **–** Literally: "Righteous Ones". Pharisaic sect founded in the 18th Century by the *Ba'al Shem-Tov.* Each *Hasidic* sect focuses around a single Rabbi dubbed "Rebbe." *Hasidim* spend much of their time engaged in so-called mystical pursuits and superstitions, especially Kaballah and prayer to dead *Hasidic* saints. For example, a major *Hasidic* event is the annual prayer pilgrimage to the grave of Rabbi Nachman of Braslav in Uman, Ukraine.

Hebraisms **–** Hebrew thought patters translated literally into another language such as Greek.

Hebrew Scripturalist **–** English translation of the term "Karaite." Someone who accepts and adheres to the Hebrew Scriptures (Old Testament).

Hebrew Syntax **–** Rules of how a Hebrew sentence is structured. These rules often differ from English syntax thereby presenting problems in translating ancient Hebrew.

Hermeneutical Interpretation **–** Another name for *Midrashic Interpretation.*

Hillel **–** Also called, "Hillel the Babylonian". Hillel immigrated to Israel from Babylonia in about 20 BCE and became the leader of one of the two major Pharisaic factions. Hillel's faction, the House of Hillel, was locked in constant struggle with the House of Shammai. The House of Shammai was wiped out in the Jewish Revolt in 66–74 CE and as a result modern Pharisees primarily continue the ways of the House of Hillel. Hillel is best-known for his seven rules of *midrashic interpretation.* Hillel the Babylonian was the ancestor of Hillel II who, according to Rabbinic tradition, invented the modern Rabbinic calendar in 359 CE.

Homiletical Interpretation **–** Another name for *Midrashic Interpretation.*

House of Hillel **–** See *Hillel.*

House of Shammai **–** See *Shammai.*

Howard, George **–** Scholar at Mercer University in Georgia who re-discovered Shem-Tov's Hebrew Matthew in the 1980s. Howard's primary accomplishment was to dispel the misconception that Shem-Tov's Hebrew Matthew was the same as the DuTillet and Münster versions of Matthew, which are apparently Hebrew translations from the Greek and/or Latin. Once Howard showed that Shem-Tov's Hebrew Matthew differed from those translations, it could be studied in its own right.

Inquisition **–** Catholic institution that coordinated systematic persecution of Jews in the Middle Ages.

Jerusalem Talmud **–** Talmud written in Tiberias and completed around 350 CE. Also known as the *Palestinian Talmud.*

Jesus **–** Commonly the English translation of "Yeshua." This name comes from the Greek IESOUS, not the Hebrew Yeshua.

Joseph Caro **–** (1488–1575) – A Sephardic Rabbi expelled from Spain in 1492. In Safed, Israel, Caro wrote the *Shulchan Aruch* a detailed guide to daily Pharisaic living.

Josephus **–** (c. 37—101 CE) – Josephus Flavius, Pharisee who witnessed the destruction of the Second Temple by the Romans. After the Jewish Revolt of 66–74 CE, Josephus wrote down a history of "The Jewish War" against Rome and later a more complete history of Israel called "Antiquities of the Jews." Before the discovery of the Dead Sea Scrolls, the writings of Josephus were the primary contemporary source for knowledge of late Second Temple Judaism.

Joshua ben Perahjah **–** Leading Pharisee Rabbi. According to Talmudic legend, the Pharisee teacher of Yeshua of Nazareth. Rabbi Joshua lived in the late 2nd Century BCE so it is unlikely he could have been Yeshua's teacher.

Judah the Prince, Rabbi **–** Leading Pharisaic leader who compiled the Mishnah in about 210 CE.

Kara **–** Ancient Hebrew word for the Hebrew Scriptures ("Old Testament").

Karaites **–** Name given to Jews who adhere to the Hebrew Scriptures as the sole source of divine instruction. See also *Hebrew Scripturalists.*

Kippah **–** Head-covering worn by modern Pharisees. According to Rabbinical law it is forbidden for a male to walk 4 cubits without a head-covering.

Kirkisani **–** 10th Century Karaite sage who lived in Kirkisan, Iraq.

Learned Commandments of Men **–** Phrase in Isaiah 29:13 describing laws invented by men. Yeshua and the Karaites applied this term to the laws of the Pharisees.

Levirate Marriage **–** Torah requirement to marry the widow of a kinsman who died without having children (Deuteronomy 25:5—10). Judah performed the levirate requirement with Tamar (Genesis 38:8, 26) as did Boaz with Ruth (Ruth 4:5).

Lubavitch **–** A sect of *Hasidim* originating in Eastern Europe. Also known as "Chabad." Many Lubavitchers have proclaimed their recently deceased Rebbe, *Menachem Mendel Schneerson*, to be the Messiah.

Ma'asim **–** Literally: "works, deeds". Pharisaic term referring to precedents of the Rabbis that provide a source for Pharisaic rulings. Also, rulings made based on these precedents.

Maimonides – 12th Century CE Pharisee theologian and Talmudic scholar whose writings shaped modern Orthodox Judaism.

Man-Made Laws – See *Takanot.*

Midrash – One of the pillars of the Oral Law written down from the 2nd to the 9th Centuries CE. Midrash is generally arranged as a running commentary on biblical verses, as opposed to the Mishnah and Talmud which are arranged by topic.

Midrashic Interpretation – Pharisaic name for the systematic irrational interpretation of Scripture. Also known as *derash, homiletical interpretation, hermeneutic interpretation.*

Mikra – Along with *Kara*, *Hebrew Scriptures*, and *Old Testament*, another name for the *Tanach.* The name is derived from Nehemiah 8:8.

Minhag – See *Custom.*

Mishnah – One of the pillars of the Oral Law, the Mishnah contains the discussions in the Pharisaic academies up until the time it was written down in about 200 CE by Rabbi Judah the Prince.

Mishnaic Hebrew – Dialect of Hebrew in which the Mishnah is written. This dialect was spoken in Israel in late Second Temple times and survived as a spoken language at least until the mid-2nd Century CE. The Dead Sea Scrolls and Shem-Tov's Hebrew Matthew are written in a variation of Mishnaic Hebrew.

Misnagdim – Literally: "Opponents". Pharisaic movement that beginning in 18th Century Europe opposed the new innovations of the *Hasidim.* Before the invention of *Hasidism* in the 18th Century, Misnagdim had no reason to call themselves "Opponents."

Modern Hebrew – Dialect of Hebrew spoken in modern Israel. Modern Hebrew differs significantly both from Biblical Hebrew and the Hebrew spoken in the First Century CE.

Mosaic Authority – Pharisaic doctrine claiming the Rabbis have the exclusive authority to interpret Scripture, supposedly deriving from an unbroken chain of ordination from Moses.

Moses' Seat – Symbol of Mosaic Authority, either a literal chair in the synagogue from which the rabbi would teach or metaphorically the rabbi sitting in place of Moses.

Moshe Isserles – 16th Century Rabbinical leader who annotated Joseph Caro's *Shulchan Aruch* with the traditions of the Ashkenazim.

Mt. Gerizim **–** Mountain in northern Israel near Shechem (Nablus) where the Samaritans still worship on an ancient High Place. Unlike the Samaritans, Jews (both Pharisees and Karaites) reject Mt. Gerizim and instead consider the chosen place to be Jerusalem.

Old Testament **–** Christian name for the *Tanach* (also called: *Hebrew Scriptures*, *Mikra*, and *Kara*).

Oral Law **–** Body of information which the Pharisees claim was revealed to Moses orally on Mt. Sinai. The Oral Law was written down in the form of the Mishnah, Talmud, and Midrash.

Oral Torah **–** Another name for the *Oral Law.*

Orthodox Jews **–** Modern name for the Pharisees.

Oven of Achnai **–** A name for the story about Rabbi Eliezer ben Hyrcanus and the Rabbis. The story of Rabbi Eliezer holds a central place in Pharisaic theology.

Palestinian Talmud **–** See *Jerusalem Talmud.*

Papias **–** (c. 60–130 CE) – "Church Father" who lived in Asia Minor. He studied under John who wrote the Gospel of John. Papias reports matter-of-factly that the Gospel of Matthew was written in Hebrew and that the translations of this book into other languages were known to be bad translations.

Pharisaic Judaism **–** See *Pharisees.*

Phariseeism **–** Religion of the Pharisees.

Pharisees **–** Jewish sect founded in the 2nd Century BCE. The primary doctrine of the sect is the belief in the "Oral Law," a secret revelation that Moses allegedly received at Mt. Sinai. Modern "Orthodox" Judaism is the direct continuation of ancient Phariseeism and medieval Rabbanism.

Rabban **–** Literally: "our Rabbi" (Aramaic). Ancient title for leading rabbis.

Rabbanism **–** Medieval name for the Pharisees. This term is used by Rabbinical sages such as Rabbi Ovadiah of Bartenoro in his *Travels to the Land of Israel* (1488).

Rabbanites **–** Medieval name for Pharisees.

Rabbi **–** Literally: "Great One". Title given to ancient teachers. Pharisee theology turned this into a term for a teacher with Mosaic authority. In the theology of the Pharisees, every rabbi is endowed with ordination supposedly stretching in an unbroken chain back to Moses.

Rabbinical Authority – Pharisaic doctrine that the Rabbis have absolute authority in religious affairs. The Pharisees believe that their authority on earth even outweighs the authority of God.

Rabbinical Jews – Modern name for the Pharisees.

Rabbinical Laws – Another name for *takanot*, laws enacted by the Rabbis.

Rashi – (1040–1105) – Also known as Rabbi Solomon ben Isaac. Pharisaic bible commentator whose commentaries are considered canonical by modern Pharisees.

Rav Ashi – Pharisaic sage who, together with Ravina, is credited with the compilation of the Babylonian Talmud around 500 CE.

Ravina – Pharisaic sage who is credited with the compilation of the Babylonian Talmud in around 500 CE together with Rav Ashi.

Rebbe – See *Hasidic Rebbe.*

Sabbath – Seventh day of the week.

Sadducees – Jewish movement in late Second Temple times who adhered to the Tanach alone. Some later Sadducees denied the future resurrection of the dead.

Samaritans – Non-Israelites settled in Samaria by the Assyrian kings in the 8th Century BCE after the exile of the Ten Northern Tribes.

Schneerson, Rabbi Menachem Mendel – 1902–1994. *Hasidic* Rebbe, leader of the Lubavitch sect. Many of his followers have proclaimed him to be the Messiah. Ironically, this belief has been strengthened after his death.

Scripturalist – See *Hebrew Scripturalist.*

Secularists – Israeli Jews who reject religion as a central part of their lives. About 70% of Israelis are secularists.

Semitisms – Semitic thought patterns (Hebrew or Aramaic), translated into a non-Semitic language such as Greek.

Sephardim – Jews from Islamic lands. Sephardim have their own traditions that differ from those of the Ashkenazim. Many Sephardim descend from Jews expelled from Spain in 1492.

Septuagint – Greek translation of the Tanach (Old Testament). The original Septuagint was translated in the 3rd Century BCE. However, the Septuagint translation underwent many revisions and with the exception of a few fragments from the Dead Sea Scrolls, the version we have today is from 4th Century CE Christian hands.

Shammai – Leader of the House of Shammai, one of the two main Pharisaic factions beginning about 20 BCE. The House of Shammai was in constant struggle with the rival Pharisaic faction, the House of Hillel. The House of Shammai was largely wiped out during the Jewish Revolt of 66–74 CE. See also *Hillel.*

Shem-Tov Ibn Shaprut – 14th Century Jewish rabbi who wrote the book Even Bochan which contains a Hebrew version of Matthew as an appendix. As a result, this Hebrew version of Matthew has become known as "Shem-Tov's Hebrew Matthew."

Shem-Tov's Hebrew Matthew – A Hebrew version of the Gospel of Matthew preserved as an appendix in a 14th Century Jewish polemical work written by Shem-Tov Ibn Shaprut. Long believed to be a translation from the Greek or Latin, this Hebrew version of Matthew has recently been shown to contain original readings that would not be found in a translation from Greek or Latin.

Shulchan Aruch – Rabbinical treatise containing legal decisions and traditions that modern Pharisees consider legally binding. The book was written by Joseph Caro in 16th Century Safed, Israel and later annotated by Moshe Isserles of Krakow, Poland.

Skullcap – See *Kippah.*

Sons of Zadok – Another name for the Sadducees. The phrase appears in Ezekiel 40:46; 44:15; 48:11.

Synoptic Gospels – Name for the first three Gospels (Matthew, Mark, and Luke) which contain parallel passages.

Tabernacles – See *Feast of Booths.*

Takanot – "Enactments". Hebrew word to describe laws enacted by the Pharisees.

Talmud – Collection of discussions from the Pharisaic academies, primary on the meaning of the Mishnah. Also known by the Aramaic name *Gemara.* See *Babylonian Talmud, Jerusalem Talmud.*

Talmudism – Early Medieval name for the Pharisees.

Talmudists – Early Medieval name for the Pharisees.

Tanach – also ***Tanakh***. Modern Jewish name for the "Old Testament." In old Hebrew the name was *Kara* or *Mikra.* The name Tanach [also: Tanakh] is an acronym for: **T**orah (Law), **N**evi'im (Prophets), **Ch**etuvim Kedoshim [or: **K**hetuvim Kedoshim] (Holy Writings).

Tiberias – Town on the western shore of the Sea of Galilee in northern Israel. The Jerusalem Talmud was actually written in Tiberias.

Torah – The five books of Moses: Genesis, Exodus, Leviticus, Numbers, Deuteronomy. Torah is usually translated as "Law" but it literally means "instruction."

Traditions of the Elders – Another name for *takanot.*

Two Torahs – Pharisaic doctrine that Moses received an Oral Torah alongside the written Torah.

Washing the Hands – Pharisaic law requiring a ritual washing of the hands and an accompanying blessing before each meal.

Word Puns – Use of similar sounding Hebrew words to create a beautiful literary texture or sometimes to emphasize a point.

Yehovah – Name of the God of Israel. In Hebrew written *YHWH* יהוה.

Ye.sh.u. – A derogatory corruption of Yeshua's name used by many Jews. This epithet is an acronym standing for "may his name and memory be blotted out."

Yeshua – The Hebrew form of the name Jesus. Yeshua is a Second Temple abbreviation of Yehoshua, the Hebrew form of Joshua.

YHWH – Yehovah, the God of Israel.

Zadok – First high priest to serve in Solomon's Temple. His descendants became known as the Sons of Zadok, or Sadducees.

Bibliography

W.C. Allen, *A Critical and Exegetical Commentary on the Gospel According to S. Matthew*, New York 1907

"Beit Yoseph" = Joseph Caro [16th Century], *Beit Yoseph* [Commentary on *Tur*] in: Ya'akov Ben Asher, *Tur*, Jerusalem 1990

E. Ben Yehudah, *A Complete Dictionary of Ancient and Modern Hebrew*, Jerusalem 1951 [Hebrew]

"Bi'ur Halachah" = Israel Meir Kagan (Chafetz Chaim) [20th Century], *Bi'ur Halachah*, in: *Mishnah Berurah* [commentary on Shulchan Aruch] [Hebrew]

F. Blass and A. Debrunner, *A Greek Grammar of the New Testament and Other Early Christian Literature*, University of Chicago 1961

"Chidushei Ramban" = Moses ben Nachman [13th Century], *Chidushei Ramban*, Or Olam Society, Jerusalem 1972 [Hebrew]

W. Chomsky, "What was the Jewish Vernacular During the Second Commonwealth?", *Jewish Quarterly Review* 42 (1951–1952) pp. 193–212

"Cruse Translation" = Eusebius of Caesarea [4th Century], *The Ecclesiastical History of Eusebius Pamphilus*, translated by C.F. Cruse, Grand Rapids, Michigan 1971

Daniel al-Kumisi [9th Century Karaite sage], "The Epistle to the Dispersion", in: L. Nemoy, "The Pseudo-Qumisian Sermon to the Karaites", *Proceedings of the American Academy for Jewish Research* 43 (1976) pp. 49–105 [Hebrew and English]

W.C. Davies and D.C. Allison, *A Critical and Exegetical Commentary on the Gospel according to Saint Matthew: Vol. 3 [Matthew XIX–XXVIII] (International Critical Commentary)*, T. & T. Clark, Edinburgh 1997

"Deferrari Translation" = Eusebius of Caesarea [4th Century], *Ecclesiastical History*, translated by R.J. Deferrari, Catholic University of America Press, Washington 1953

J.D. Eisenstein, *Ozar Wikuhim: A Collection of Polemics and Disputations with Introduction, Annotations and Index*, New York 1928 [Hebrew]

E.J. Epp, "Ancient Texts and Versions of the New Testament", in: *New Interpreter's Bible: Vol. VIII*, Abingdon Press, Nashville 1995, pp. 1–11

Exodus Rabbah, translated by S.M. Lehrman, Soncino Press, London and New York 1983

J.C. Fenton, *Saint Matthew (The Pelican Gospel Commentaries)*, Penguin Books 1963

L. Garshowitz, "Shem Tov ben Isaac Ibn Shaprut's Gospel of Matthew", in: *The Frank Talmage Memorial Volume I*, ed. B. Walfish, Haifa 1993, pp. 297–322

"Goldin Translation" = S. Ganzfried [19th Century], *Code of Jewish Law: Kitzur Shulhan Aruch*, translated by H.E. Goldin, Hebrew Publishing Company, New York 1961

J.M. Grintz, "Hebrew as the Spoken and Written Language in the Last Days of the Second Temple", *Journal of Biblical Literature* 79 (1960) pp. 32–47

D.A. Hagner, *Matthew 14–28 (Word Biblical Commentary)*, Word Books Publisher, Dallas 1995

"Hammer Translation" = *Sifre: A Tannaitic Commentary on the Book of Deuteronomy*, translated by R. Hammer, Yale University Press, New Haven and London 1986

W. Horbury, "The Hebrew Text of Matthew in Shem Tob ibn Shaprut's Eben Bohan", in: Davies and Allison, pp. 729–738

G. Howard, "The Tetragram and the New Testament", *Journal of Biblical Literature* 96 (1977) pp. 63–83

G. Howard, "Shem-Tob's Hebrew Matthew", *Proceedings of the Ninth World Congress of Jewish Studies (Jerusalem, August 4–12, 1985): Division A*, Jerusalem 1986, pp. 223–230

G. Howard, "Was the Gospel of Matthew Originally Written in Hebrew?", *Bible Review* 2,4 (1986) pp. 15–25

G. Howard, *The Gospel of Matthew According to a Primitive Hebrew Text*, Mercer University Press, Macon, Georgia 1987

G. Howard, "The Pseudo-Clementine Writings and Shem-Tob's Hebrew Matthew", *New Testament Studies* 40 (1994) pp. 622–628

G. Howard, *Hebrew Gospel of Matthew*, Mercer University Press, Macon, Georgia 1995

G. Howard, "Shem-Tob's Hebrew Matthew and Early Jewish Christianity", *Journal for the Study of the New Testament* 70 (1998) pp. 3–20

G. Howard, "A Response to William L. Petersen's Review of Hebrew Gospel of Matthew", *TC: A Journal of Biblical Textual Criticism 4* (1999) [E-Journal], http://purl.org/TC

"Ben Isaiah and Sharfman Translation" = *The Pentateuch and Rashi's Commentary: A Linear Translation into English*, translated by A. Ben Isaiah and B. Sharfman, New York 1949

M. Jastrow, *Dictionary of Talmud Babli, Yerushalmi, Midrashic Literature and Targumim*, New York 1950

G.A. Kiraz, *Comparative Edition of the Syriac Gospels*, Leiden 1996

"Kirkisani" = B. Chiesa and W. Lockwood, *Ya'qub al-Qirqisani on Jewish Sects and Christianity*, Frankfurt am Main 1984 [10th Century Karaite sage]

"*Kitzur Shulchan Aruch*" = S. Ganzfried [19th Century], *Kizzur Schulchan Aruch*, Basel 1965 [Hebrew and German]

"Lake Translation" = Eusebius of Caesarea [4th Century], *The Ecclesiastical History (Loeb Classical Library)*, translated by K. Lake, London 1926 [Greek and English]

G.M. Lamsa, *New Testament Origins*, Chicago and New York 1947

H.G. Liddell and R. Scott, *A Greek-English Lexicon*, Clarendon Press, Oxford 1968

"LXX" = A. Rahlfs (ed.), *Septuaginta*, Deutsche Bibelgesellschaft, Stuttgart 1979

"Marcus Translation" = Josephus Flavius [1st Century CE], *Josephus, Vol. VII (Loeb Classical Library)*, translated by R. Marcus, Harvard University Press, London 1958 [Greek and English]

B.M. Metzger, *The Early Versions of the New Testament*, Oxford 1977

J.P. Migne (ed.), *Patrologiae Cursus Completus: Series Graeca*, Paris 1886 (Microfiche Edition, Interdocumentation, Zug, Switzerland 1970)

"*Mishnah Berurah*" = I.M. Kagan (Chafetz Chaim) [20th Century], *Mishnah Berurah*, Jerusalem and New York 1972 [commentary on Shulchan Aruch; printed together with *Shulchan Aruch* and *Bi'ur Halachah*] [Hebrew]

Moses Maimonides, *Introduction to the Mishnah*, Jerusalem 1992 [Hebrew]

Ross K. Nichols, "The Seat of Moses: A Note on Matthew 23:2–3 According to Shem Tob's Hebrew Matthew" [online study], *http://www.ancientpaths.org/*

Pesikta DeRav Kahana, D. Mandelbaum (ed.), New York 1987

W.L. Petersen, "*The Gospel of Matthew according to a Primitive Hebrew Text*, by George Howard" (book review), *Journal of Biblical Literature* 108 (1989) pp. 722–726

W.L. Petersen, "The *Vorlage* of Shem-Tob's 'Hebrew Matthew'", *New Testament Studies* 44 (1998) pp. 490–512

W.L. Petersen, "Some Observations on a Recent Edition of and Introduction to Shem-Tob's 'Hebrew Matthew'", *TC: A Journal of Biblical Textual Criticism* 4 (1999) [E-Journal], http://purl.org/TC

M.A. Powell, "Do and Keep What Moses Says (Matthew 23:2–7)", Journal of Biblical Literature 114 (1995) pp. 419–435

L.Y. Rahmani, "Stone Synagogue Chairs: Their Identification, Use and Significance", *Israel Exploration Journal* 40 (1990) pp. 192–214

"Rashi" = Solomon ben Isaac [11th Century] in: *Torat Chayim*, Mosad Harav Cook, Jerusalem 1993 [Rabbinic Bible commentary] [Hebrew]

I. Renov, "The Seat of Moses", *Israel Exploration Journal* 5 (1955) pp. 262–267

Y. Rosental, "Jewish Criticism of the New Testament from the 13th Century", in: *Studies in Jewish Bibliography, History and Literature: Y. Kiov Jubilee Volume*, Y. Berlin (ed.), New York 1972, pp. 123–139 [Hebrew]

"Rosner Translation" = *Maimonides' Introduction to His Commentary on the Mishnah*, translated by F. Rosner, Jason Aronson, Inc., Northvale, New Jersey and London 1995

R.F. Shedinger, "The Textual Relationship Between "P45" and Shem-Tob's Hebrew Matthew", *New Testament Studies* 43 (1997) pp. 58–71

R.F. Shedinger, "A Further Consideration of the Textual Nature of Shem-Tob's Hebrew Matthew", *Catholic Bible Quarterly* 61,4 (1999) pp. 686–694

Siddur Rinat Yisrael: Nusach Sefarad, Sh. Tal (ed.), Jerusalem 1984 [Hebrew]

Sifre on Deuteronomy, L. Finkelstein (ed.), New York 1969 [Hebrew]

"Shulchan Aruch" = Joseph Caro [16th Century], *Shulchan Aruch*, in: *Mishnah Berurah* [Hebrew]

"Soncino Translation" = *Hebrew-English Edition of the Babylonian Talmud: Sanhedrin*, translated by J. Schachter and H. Freedman, Soncino Press, London 1969

H.L. Strack and G. Stemberger, *Introduction to the Talmud and Midrash*, translated by M. Bockmuehl, T. & T. Clark, Edinburgh 1991

E.L. Sukenik, *Ancient Synagogues in Palestine and Greece*, London 1934

N. Turner, *A Grammar of New Testament Greek, Vol. IV: Style*, T. & T. Clark, Edinburgh 1976

"Whiston Translation" = Josephus Flavius [1st Century CE], *Complete Works of Josephus*, translated by W. Whiston, Kregel Publications, Grand Rapids, Michigan 1981

M. Whittaker, *New Testament Greek Grammar: An Introduction*, SCM Press Ltd 1969

Ya'akov ben Reuven, *Wars of the Lord*, Y. Rosental (ed.), Jerusalem 1973 [Hebrew]

M. Zerwick and J. Smith, *Biblical Greek Illustrated by Examples*, Rome 1977

Indices

Subject Index

S

T

V

W

Y

Z

Tanach (Old Testament) Citations

New Testament Citations

Citations of Other Ancient Sources